"*Mirror, Mirror, on the Wall* explores ways to learn to live with one's self and with others." — *Publishers Weekly*

"The author is showing us how to attain serenity by creating harmony among our many inner selves...."
— *Dr. Lucie W. Barber*
Schenectady, N.Y.

"Father Powers's method is to introduce us in imagination to our 'many selves within': the angry one, the guilty one, the afflicted one, the fearful one, the worried one—but also, the lover in us, the responsible one, the courageous one, the hopeful one, the creative one. He sets up an 'inner dialogue' with the raging passions and the dormant emotions that cause conflict, yet are pregnant with possibilities." — *Spiritual Book News*

"Father Powers tells his readers that instead of fearing or attacking the inner parts of one's self, a befriending process should begin....

"He puts meat on the bones of his ideas. He shows readers how to begin to have inner conversations. And he does it in a very honest and revealing way....

"Father Powers wants more people to talk to themselves and his suggestions could, after a few painful discoveries, lead to a great deal of serenity."
— *The Catholic Observer*

"The 12 steps toward serenity with which the book ends may be demanding, but getting it all together is worth the effort." — *Prairie Messenger*

"The final chapter focuses on 'Twelve Steps Toward Serenity.' It's a list that is worth posting in a prominent place....

"...[this] book is one to cherish."
— *St. Anthony Messenger*

Foreword by Eugene Kennedy

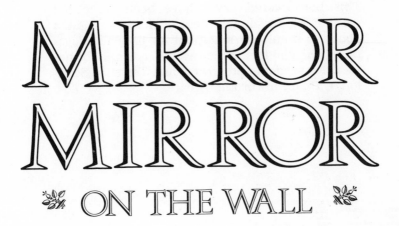

MIRROR MIRROR
❧ ON THE WALL ❧

The Art of Talking With Yourself

John Daniel Powers

TWENTY-THIRD PUBLICATIONS
Mystic, Connecticut

248
PoW

Gratitude

This book would never have been completed without the invaluable help of three very gifted people. I thank Mark Dupont for his encouragement, friendship, and counsel, Bea Smith for her intuitive wisdom and advice, and Terrence Scanlon, C.P., for his brotherly care.

Third printing 1990

Twenty-Third Publications
P.O. Box 180
Mystic, CT 06355
(203) 536-2611

ISBN 0-89622-344-2
Library of Congress Catalog Number 87-50839

Quotations from *Human Options, An Autobiographical Notebook*, by Norman Cousins, are used by permission of W.W. Norton & Company, Inc. © 1981 by Norman Cousins.

689

Dedication

To my parents, Tom and Mary
my brothers, Tom and Peter
my sisters Mary Louise, Ann Marie, Margaret Ann,
and Kathleen
I dedicate the effort and energy of this book.

Foreword

In one of the most important, yet overlooked or consistently misinterpreted, of his sayings, Jesus tells us that "the kingdom of God is within you." This book, written with the intense concern for the reader that is very different from easy reassurance or superficial manipulation, is about just this subject. It could only be written by a person well acquainted with and generously forgiving of our infirmity, a priest who has felt the strong currents running in the depths of those who have come to him for help, and who, in addition, has listened with understanding to himself at the same time. Only an individual who has come to terms with himself or herself could give us a book that bears the much sought but elusive gift of peace.

A Walkman in the ear seems the choice of many persons who want, at all costs, to drown out the already noisy environment. Those who wear such headsets, as Saul Bellow once remarked as we crossed a busy Chicago street, "will never hear the voice of God." The reason, of course, is that they cannot even overhear themselves; they are shut off from that part of their personalities in which God, more truly than at Siloe, stirs the waters of their souls. Perhaps they are not so different from the deaf people who seem to be standing at every intersection in the scriptures. The latter needed to be healed in spirit before they could listen again with any comprehension of the world or of themselves. The real miracle may not have lain in kindling life again into dead nerves, but rather in something that Jesus expressed through his understanding acceptance of them. In his presence, the deaf, yes, and the blind, too, no longer needed to be so angry or afraid. The obstacles to their hearing and seeing may have been their own long-unattended conflicts, the unhappy truths about themselves too painful to look upon, the cries of their hearts too anguished to hear.

Other people will listen to anybody but themselves, trying anything and everything in hopes that they will find the right formula, or the correct medication, to ease them of their griefs. This may, in fact, be the golden age of the charlatans who play upon human pain and longing through remedies as worthless as the elixirs that were once hawked from the back of circus wagons. The contemporary promoters of such cures frequently speak a language heavy with jargon but light in meaning, replete with promises of self-actualization, self-fulfillment, and self-realization through methods that are usually as vague in substance as the phrases of their description. Men and women simply find that they cannot live on this insubstantial nourishment, that there are hungers deeper inside them that only become sharper under doses of such distorted psychology.

Still others wait for deliverance from another planet, from friendly aliens who will descend, as in *Close Encounters of The Third Kind*, to solve our problems with their higher wisdom. Such notions of deliverance are as deceptive as those that come through spurious spiritual messengers claiming to speak the saving advice of thousand-year-old sages. It is a poignant measure of our culture's need that it should turn to Shirley MacLaine as a medium of transcendence.

The kingdom does not lie outside ourselves, nor will salvation come to us from some distant source. Just as we make pilgrimages only so that we can return home, we discover that our true spiritual journey is inward and that we must make it for ourselves. This book, so sensitive to every kind of human pain, offers us an invitation to enter that kingdom, to give names, as Adam did, to the animals within us, and to begin to know ourselves even as we are known and loved by God. Its great merit lies in its profound human understanding, in Father Powers's obviously unselfish— and unself-conscious— concern that we find true healing and peace.

Father Powers understands that the true signs of our times are such things as the unresolved anger that tingles in the air around us and the crippling fear that casts out love. Through simple but insightful dialogues he allows people to enter themselves once again, to descend without defensiveness into their own depths. I think you will come to feel that Father Powers is a friend and a good companion, a pastor of souls who knows the way and yet lets us find it for ourselves.

Eugene Kennedy

Contents

MIRROR, MIRROR ON THE WALL...

Introduction

What do we hunger for in the world today? What do we truly yearn for as the evening news bombards us each day with stories that almost curdle the blood and freeze the heart? Isn't the heart's deepest desire for personal and universal peace? Isn't serenity what we search for and peace what we long for? But where can we find even the possibility of serenity in the face of the massive social, emotional, economic, ethnic, ideological, and religious conflicts that rage throughout the world?

At times it seems impossible to find a moment's calm even in our own homes, among those we live with and love, much less find serenity in a world on the edge of chaos. How can we think of world peace when it takes every ounce of energy just to build a sense of family peace? There must be a way to live in this competitive world without being dragged through it screaming for harmony and moaning for peace. There must be way to live with our wives, husbands, children, parents, grandparents, in-laws, neighbors, and fellow workers without having constantly to fight for inner peace. There must be a more honest way to find it.

This book is about the search for serenity, the preference for peace, the hunger for inner and outer harmony. The aim of this book is to find the only real, enduring peace that can be found: serenity among your many selves, within your inner community and family.

1

If living in a competitive world is difficult and if living with one another is painful at times, then living with your self can be the most demanding challenge of all. No peace will ever be found in the world of nations, states, families, or neighbors unless it is first discovered within your own inner world of fears, worries, hopes, dreams, guilts, creative ideas, fantasies, transcendent urges and loves. If you want to build peace in the outer world, you must first demythologize your self-created inner enemies.

This book is about learning to live with the only person with whom you will share every moment of your life. The one person you will eat every meal with, cry every tear with, sleep every night with, work every day with, and pray every way with: yourself. If you can learn to live with your self, you can learn to live with anyone.

In this book I hope to share what has been opened to me, the world of the inner family. I did not write this book, however, as though I have privileged knowledge that you do not. Rather, I wrote it to remind us both of very important facts all too easily forgotten, that learning to live with, relate to, and communicate with your self is the first step in the process of learning to relate to other people and to God. If you can learn to be happy with who you truly are, you can learn to be happy with others in daily living.

If in these pages I can introduce you to some of the selves within, your inner family, then I will have accomplished something very important. If I can reveal the true source of inner harmony, while reminding you of the preference for peace that lives within you, then I will have reached a divine goal.

As one familiar with the terrain of personal and spiritual development and growth, I offer knowledge of the ways of your inner community so that, through this sharing, you may find greater personal and spiritual serenity. I will provide no light for this inner journey, however, that is not already there.

Chapter One

The Many Selves

Dietrich Bonhoeffer, a German theologian executed in 1943 for his opposition to Adolf Hitler, answers the question "Who am I?" in this way:

> *Who am I? This or the other? Am I one person today and tomorrow another? Am I both at once? A hypocrite before others, and before myself a contemptibly woe-be-gone weakling, or is something within me still like a beaten army, fleeing in disorder from victory already achieved?*[1]

If serenity is ever to be found, we must begin the search by asking the simple question, "Who am I?" Through this daring question, we will be led to the most complex of discoveries, the family within.

Who am I? I am John, I am Mary, I am Tom, I am Ann. Whatever my name is, I know that I am me. I am one person with a history lived, a present I am attempting to live in, and an unknown future I am trying to prepare for—but I am one person, one identity. Ask the question again, however, and the complexity of Bonhoeffer's response will press itself even further.

Who am I? I am a secretary, I am a plumber, I am a lawyer, a truck driver, priest, student, social worker, father, mother, spouse. But there is more to me than my job or role, more to me than what I do. So, to answer the question further, I declare that "I am kind" and "I am fearful." "I am also loving, yet I find myself angry at times." "I am joyful but I am also confused." The list goes on as I attempt to answer the simple question, "Who am I?"

I am an alcoholic, a nervous person, handicapped, an overeater, a jogger. I am a Christian, an atheist. I may describe myself by name, social roles, illness, attitudes, religious inclination, needs, physical attributes, moods, feelings, political persuasion, desires, or ideas. The list is endless as I discover the remarkable yet terrifying complexity of my many inner selves.

Although I am one person, with a sense of identity, I am also a multiplicity of moods, tendencies, memories, desires, needs, emotions, and thoughts. I am a unity of many, a variety moving toward breakdown or synthesis, a fabric of threads to be woven. I am a broken "we," a family of inner relatives connected by psyche, spirit, blood, and body. I am one person with many inner members, many selves.

Psychologists have developed an array of words to describe the dynamic of conscious and unconscious self-identities. The variety of inner characters can be called complexes, traits, temperaments, attitudes, moods, ego, id, super-ego, child, adult, parent, sub-personalities, roles, or semi-autonomous feelings. The complexity of our inner world is as vast as that of the outer world. Within us lives the power of fear and love, the potential for hate and compassion, as well as the motivation for building or tearing down. There is within each of us the preference for unity, yet the driving urge toward multiplicity. I am one, but I have many inner community members. I feel like a shattered "we" rather than a united "I."

Ignorance of the Inner World

One reason we find little serenity in life is because we too often ignore our own shifting identity, our own inner world. We take ourselves for granted until the pull and push of inner conflicts breaks through into actions we do not will.

If you resist the thought that you are one in identity yet have many inner selves, you are not alone. It is not an easy task to recognize this inner diversity. The possibility of such a multiplicity of inner characters threatens our sense of oneness. We want to simplify, not complicate, our lives. The desire for the uncomplicated is often the voice of ignorance attempting to take control. It is the arrogance of ignorant fear that prevents personal and spiritual growth.

The inner family is not only real in principle, but in our daily functioning as well. As we live we may continue to think of ourselves as merely one orderly piece, but when we look closely at our behavior we can see that we allow different aspects of who we are to operate at different times. When, for example, we meet someone we care for, we will greet him or her with a sense of joy. "It's so good to see you," we tell our friend. Five minutes later, however, we may meet someone who we feel has hurt us in some way. In response to that person we may either hide in fear or boil with anger. In these two encounters, who is it who changed? Who became the happy person one moment and the fearful or angry person the next? How we respond often depends upon what we see, not with our eyes but with our inner feeling. Friends you can meet anywhere, enemies you have to create. As David Harden writes:

> *Sight is individualized, shaped for better and for worse, by a whole household of images that find their residence within the self long before the eyes scrutinize a face or examine a new situation.*[2]

We may think we are one orderly personality when, in reality, we are constantly changing in response to what we experience. Our identity seems to shift from one mood to the next, one feeling to the next, one real expectation to the next. Psychologists, scientists, philosophers, and mystics may agree that there is an essential underlying unity deep within the unconscious; still we seem to experience far more the myriad diversities of our inner lives than the foundational unity. This is the great paradox, of being one, yet living out of many sub-personalities. It is a paradox we must live with, whether for health or for ill. If we live well with our many selves, we will discover serenity; if we ignore our inner community, we will live in a shadow world of anxiety.

If in the realm of the unconscious lives a family of complex and almost willfully motivated emotions, then it is quite a normal mode of madness to experience oneself as multi-dimensional in personality. Just because we recognize a variety of family members within, a cast of characters residing in the household of our unconscious, does not mean we are ill. Mental illness is determined to a large extent by how well we cope with our inner world of unconscious passions, feelings, and needs.

We are all neurotic to some extent, out of touch with the reality of our inner selves. We find our many selves at war with one another, divided at times by mixed motivations. This inner disunity is obvious when we look at the inconsistencies in our behavior. We say we want one thing, peace for example, yet we fight with others and our selves. Even the Christian Scriptures recognize the dangers when the inner household and kingdom are in conflict. "If a household is divided according to loyalties, that household will not survive" (Mark 3:25) and "Every kingdom divided against itself is laid waste. Any household torn by dissension falls" (Luke 11:17). Where is the reason in such conflicting behavior?

Voices in Conflict

It is estimated that there are over forty-two different wars or military conflicts going on somewhere on the globe with thousands dying or being wounded every day. If we could look inside our inner world, would we not find just as many inner conflicts, if not outright wars, being waged? Perhaps there is no body count when you fight with your many inner selves, but you can be just as wounded by inner conflicts as by any outside struggle. Even St. Paul recognizes the conflicting inner voices when he describes living with himself as though he were at war (Romans 7:19-23).

> *What happens is that I do not the good I will to do but the evil I do not intend. But if I do what is against my will, it is not I who does it but sin which dwells in me. This means that even though I want to do what is right, a law that leads to wrongdoing is always ready at hand. My inner self agrees with the Law of God but I see in my body's members another law at war with the law of my mind; this makes me the prisoner of the law of sin in my members.*

Everything we do is motivated by a mixture of competitive desires and conflicting voices. We are influenced, and perhaps even driven, by obsessive urges we do not understand and know far too little about to confront or guide.

Our every choice is motivated by a mixture of loud and soft voices speaking within our own unconscious worlds. Dr. Scott Peck in his popular book, *The Road Less Traveled*, describes for us just how vast our inner cosmos is:

> *When beginning work with a new patient, I will frequently draw a large circle. Then, at the circumference, I will draw a small niche. Pointing to the inside of the niche, I say, "That represents your conscious mind. All the rest of the*

circle, ninety-five percent or more, represents your unconscious. If you work long enough, and hard enough, to understand yourself, you will come to discover that the vast part of your mind, of which you have little awareness, contains riches beyond imagination."[3]

Far too often we believe that the "niche of consciousness" is all that we are, when in reality it is the tip of the tip of the iceberg. Below the surface of consciousness reside images and sub-personalities, driving needs, and powerful emotions. Within our unconscious lives a family of voices, a variety of psychic energies, an assembly of complexes, a community of brother urges and sister needs. Whether we are awake or asleep, our unconscious world pulsates with constant psychic activity. There is not a moment when the inner family members do not speak and, more often than not, fight for control. Like Dietrich Bonhoeffer in the earlier quote, Somerset Maugham also discovers a multitude when he looks within, wondering ultimately who the real self is.

When I look over the various parts of my character with perplexity, I recognize that I am made up of several persons and that the person that at the moment has the upper hand will inevitably give place to another. But which is the real one? All of them or none?[4]

Chapter Two

Inner Family Communication

Educator, columnist, and family specialist, Dolores Curran, writes in her well-researched and perceptive book, *Traits of a Healthy Family*, that communication and listening were

> chosen as the number one trait found in healthy families. . . .[1]

The surveys conducted by the author, as well as those taken by the National Study of Family Strengths, indicate without doubt that the most important characteristic of a healthy and growing family is the ability to talk and listen honestly.

Just as communication is the first trait of a healthy outer family of brothers, sisters, husband, wife, neighbors, or friends, so it is the primary tool for living well with the inner family. To the extent you are unable to communicate with your many inner selves, to that extent do you find outer communication difficult. To the extent you are ignorantly and fearfully silent with your inner family, to that extent do you neglect your outer family. Healthy inner family communication and listening leads to healthy outer community sharing.

When we talk and listen to God, we call it prayer. When we talk with others we call it conversation or dialogue. Some think talking to and listening to yourself is insane. Properly understood, however, it is truly a disci-

plined art that can build an atmosphere of personal serenity. Learning to live with our selves can be a painful
process but life is far more painful when we avoid the realities that live within. If we want to learn to live with
our selves, we must learn how to talk to and listen to our
many feelings, moods, urges, thoughts, tendencies, attitudes, desires, and needs. By confronting our many inner selves with love, we can learn the art of "inner conversation," or to use a more technical description,
"intra-communication."

To develop and build a healthy inner family atmosphere, you must work at being honest with yourself. You
must recognize what truly lives within you: the needs,
feelings, desires, attitudes, cravings, and obsessions that
are a part of your inner world. Not only must you honestly recognize your inner feelings and needs, you must also
"put them on the table," talk with them and get to know
them very well.

Every person has within the same potential for fear
and hunger for love. No one is without feelings. At times
emotions and needs may be so buried in repression that
they seem almost lost, but the potential for every human
emotion is always present. Honestly admitting that you
are like all other men and women, in that you also have
frustrated feelings and powerful desires, is the first step
toward inner family communication. Just as you cannot
have a conversation with another person until you recognize his or her presence, so too, you cannot honestly
talk with and listen to yourself until you admit that there
is something or someone alive within.

To say "I feel angry" gives you the opportunity to
converse with and listen to this emotion. By admitting
that anger has become so strong that it has for a time
taken over your identity, your I-ness, gives you the opportunity to do something about the anger. Recognition
of how you feel and what you need can lead to honest inner conversation and synthesis. To communicate with

your inner family members, however, you must first admit into your consciousness the reality of your feelings and the existence of your needs. For freedom's sake, you must consciously confront what passions you have made into inner enemies in order to liberate your inner friends.

Let Be What Is

Another guideline for inner family dialogue, or intra-communication, is to withhold judgment concerning how you feel or what you desire. If you meet another person and immediately decide that you do not like that person, for whatever reason, the opportunity to become friends is thrown away. Your negative judgment has become an obstacle not only to communication but to possible intimacy. If you do the same with your inner feelings and needs, deciding that you do not like feeling fearful or that you do not like to feel in need, haven't you also tossed away the chance to befriend these very real selves and sub-personalities?

If you truly want to "get your head together," "find the real you," or perhaps better phrased, "learn to live with your many inner family selves," then communication with your selves is essential. Making friends with your many inner selves— love, hate, worry, courage, the need to be loved— demands a deep, abiding self-respect. You can never come to know and care for someone unless you begin with a respect for who they are. So it is with coming to know and live with the passions and needs that reside within you. If you respect how you feel, you will grow in freedom; if you do not, you will be creating your own inner adversaries.

Treat your passions and needs as though they were people living within you. Dignify them with respect and care; listen with openness and understanding and they will learn to give you the best of themselves.

Imagine Your Many Selves

A constant activity goes on in your unconscious. It is the seeming chaotic, symbolic, and in its own way, logical, doing of image making. Humans are image makers, driven by the need to organize what is seen, categorize what is thought, and label what is felt. Every picture that rises from the unconscious in a dream or fantasy and every word that you form prove that your imagination is continually at work. Through your ability to imagine you can come to know more and more about yourself, the world and, if you choose, God as well. Imagination can be an accurate way of knowing. As you represent in word or picture the experience that is felt to be important, you can come to understand that experience in a fuller way. Imagination is not just a fantasy world to escape to, but rather a place where you can face your many selves.

On a very special private retreat some years ago, I had a radical experience of my inner family. With the guidance of a wise and well-trained director, I met, through my active imagination, various members of my inner family. This is how I imagined some of my selves.

During the five days of seclusion, I was instructed to draw on paper any strong feelings, needs, or passions I felt. When you spend long periods of time alone, the inner world takes on a reality that is at other times smothered by external activity. Within hours of my solitude, I began to draw. The purpose of this was to conceptualize the feelings and passions that arose from my unconscious. What actually took place was an inner family meeting. By drawing my feelings, I brought them before myself in a concrete and conceptualized way. I imaged in color and shape how I felt. The so-called inner adversary feelings of anger and anxiety, as well as my need to be loved and my need to control, were given a name, a size, and a shading. Each drawing expressed a partial image of my personality. As drawing after drawing flowed, some sixteen in all before I ended the retreat, I came to understand myself, my personality, and my inner community in a new way. By drawing my feelings and needs, I had articulated through my imagination a fuller description of myself. As David Harden indicates:

> A sense of identity is the result of a process of imaginings; it is simply a cluster of images that inform the consciousness of the self. . .On the works of the imagination everything else depends, and among its works the most important are the images of the self that it offers us for interpreting our nature and possibilities and perils.[2]

Every counselor, therapist, or analyst knows that for mental health and psychological balance the ability to imagine is an invaluable tool. Through the imagination, you can confront your fears with respect, transforming them in the process from emotions falsely perceived as deadly enemies into the creative friends they are. Image making is ultimately for the sake of idol breaking. All too often we make what we feel and what we need into idols to be obeyed and not passions to live with and grow through. When you give too much power or over identify with a part of yourself—a feeling of anger or mood of loneliness—you allow it to become the whole of yourself. Rather than saying, "I have lonely feelings," you say, "I am lonely." You identify who you are with how you feel. In doing so, you grant to an emotion the power to move, direct, and control your life.

Will Power

Serenity with your many selves can be found, if you get out of your own way. The crux is whether you use or abuse the capacity called will power. Perhaps the most misunderstood of abilities is the capacity of intentional and attentive will power. It is usually misunderstood as a thing to be measured. You either have a great deal of it and if you do you can control how you feel and act, or you lack a certain amount of it and find yourself out of control, behaving in ways you do not choose, feeling emotions you do not want. Understood in such a way, will power becomes a means for self-domination and self-mastery, a harsh and cruel tyrant that keeps you in line.

The will, however, is not a thing to be measured in degrees, nor is it merely a tool for negative self-discipline. The will is a capacity, an ability to act with deliberate and creative choice. Will power is to be seen as the foundation of choice, not control; deliberation, not domination; attention, not command. The capacity of will is not "strong" or "weak" but is developed through the process of conscious learning. Understood correctly, will power is not a power "over" but a power "for" positive choice; not a dominating force that imposes discipline from outside but a deliberate choice for action. Will power is not an imposition of authority, but rather it allows the power and preference for the best to direct actions. The will guides with love; it does not dominate with aggressive force. Will power is a positive capacity for serenity.

Befriend Your Selves

The acquired ability of "will power for life" is learned in the process of compassionately and attentively befriending your inner selves. If you desire "will power for life," you must have compassion and understanding for the very feelings and sub-personalities that cause you the most problems. The best known are: The Angry One, The Guilty One, The Addicted One, The Worrying One, and The Fearful One. Coventry Patmore has described well how you can best learn to live with, relate to, and communicate with your selves:

> Great is his happiness and safety who has beaten all his enemies, but far greater his to whom they have become friends and allies. Happy he

who has conquered his passions, but far happier he whose servants and friends they have become. The reconciled passions are the sure mercies of David.[3]

If you want freedom from the passions that drive you and the feelings that dominate you, you must "give the devil his due": recognize and respect the feelings and passions as inner realities that need to be heard. We have heard that to build healthy inter-personal relationships with the outer family, you must spend quality time with each member, giving attention and affection to each. The same is true in intra-personal relationships within your selves. If you do not listen to the needs your feelings voice, you will condemn yourself to their control. If you do not hear the noises of your passions, you will imprison yourself in their demands. If you do not recognize your emotions and needs as your own, you are doomed either to turn them into adversaries or to project them onto others. Friendship is built upon mutual respect, attentive listening, and time together. If you do not accept and befriend your basic human emotions, you merely give them the power to dominate and master your inner life, and you make of them enemies that must one day be fought. Swiss psychiatrist Carl Jung clearly recommended how we are to deal with the feelings and needs that have been ignored, repressed, and warped into inner adversaries.

That I feed the hungry, that I forgive an insult, that I love my enemy in the name of Christ, all these are undoubtedly great virtues. What I do to the least of my brethren, that I do unto Christ. But what if I should discover that the least among them all, the poorest of all the beggars, the most imprudent of all the offenders, the very enemy himself—that these are within me and that I myself stand in need of

*the alms of kindness— that I myself am the ene-
my that must be loved. What then?*[4]

In the following chapters I will not only introduce
you to some of your sub-personalities, but I will also talk
with some of them. When people who care about each
other get together they frequently spend their time
sharing their joys and sorrows, needs and concerns. I
will dialogue with the inner family members we share,
the inner fears, guilts, worries, and angers that can possess us, as well as the creative friends that can guide us
toward health. Inner serenity can grow through such
sharing.

Chapter Three

Befriending Inner Adversaries

When there are international conflicts and disagreements, the way to resolution is either through negotiation or war. Whether there are differences of opinion or division on a family level, the same is true. Either you talk with and listen to your brother, sister, father, husband, wife, or mother or you build for war. Family problems not talked about can build to the point where the only option left is all-out nuclear divorce. Dialogue is the only way to resolve conflict without condemning the other. Problems ignored, in the hopes that they will go away, become bigger problems left for another day.

Every counsellor's or therapist's office is filled with men and women who do not know how to talk to, listen to, and negotiate not only with others but more importantly with their many inner selves. Counsellors and therapists do the work that could have and, without judging, should have been done years before in the natural education process of the child. As children we should have learned how to dialogue with our most powerful feelings and needs, for it is then that our imaginations are most capable of dealing with the realities of our inner psychic world. At the very least, as children we may have allowed our needs and emotions to become ghosts and goblins that hide under the bed. All too often, we adults seal our passions and needs in the closet of our unconscious, burying them in ignorance.

The Door to the Unconscious

In order to appreciate the concept of the family and community within, and the technique of talking to your selves, or intra-dialogue, imagine the following. You are standing in your bedroom, probably the most personal place you have. There your conscious personality sleeps while your unconscious selves continue their activity. Now that you are an adult, you can open the closet door, behind which live the most fearsome of feelings, the deepest of hurts, as well as the most sublime emotions of joy and the most potent of creative abilities. Not only does the closet of your unconscious contain the foes you fear but also the friends and angels you cherish as your own. As you reach for the handle of the closet door, you notice the key that must be turned to open the door. This key is your desire for freedom, your knowledge that it is better to know and face the truth than remain in ignorance. To turn the key of courage will certainly bring pain, but it will also open up the possibility of serenity. As you turn the key, the door begins to open. You do not want it to open too quickly, however, for fear of being overwhelmed by the demons and angels that live in the closet of your unconscious. As the closet door opens, only one of the many inner selves will come out at a time. If too many sub-personalities burst forth at once from the closet, you would not be able to cope with them, learn their names, and listen to their stories. Therefore, only one inner family member steps out into the soft light of your bedroom. Who is it?

The Angry One

Anger is the feeling of being irritated, irked, annoyed, "teed-off," resentful, hostile, and aggressive. It is one of the most powerful, complex, stimulating, and creative emotions; yet it is also the most potentially destructive.

The feelings of anger that live in the closet of your unconscious can be friends that help your relationships grow, or foes that destroy friendship. Whether your anger is friend or foe depends to a large degree upon your respect for this necessary human emotion and whether your anger flows from love or is born of resentful hurt.

Almost all of us have been taught in a wide variety of conscious and unconscious ways that anger, so closely related with hurt, should be avoided at all cost. Repressed anger, however, becomes a demon that takes possession in outbursts of temper and acts of hostility. Because feelings of anger almost always have a powerful aura of danger attached to them, they are often buried behind a smile or hidden inside a compulsive personality waiting for a heart attack.

Even our language betrays our fear of anger's power. It is described in images of heat: "hot under the collar," "boiling mad," "slow burn," or "hot-blooded." Perhaps we use such descriptive images because we know that fire burns and everyone has been taught at a very young age never to play with fire.

Anger repressed is simply anger awaiting expression. If you do not give it a voice, by listening to your true feelings of anger, it will find its own way out of hiding. When angry feelings are not given an appropriate expression, they will find inappropriate outlets. If you do not cope with it constructively, it will either express its power inward, creating havoc on the body and soul, or express itself outward at others, even God. Directing anger inward can cause depression or psychosomatic illness. Directing it outward can cause physical or emotional violence.

The capacity to experience anger is a biological gift, an endowment. It serves as a protector from hurt and as a voice against injustice. When it is ignored, however, and left to fester within the closet of the unconscious it can grow to terrifying and destructive proportions. Anger arises typically when someone has threatened something or someone you care for as your own. Anyone can feel the emotion of anger, but according to Aristotle:

> *The one who gets angry at the right things and the right people, and also in the right way and at the right time and for the right length of time, should be commended. . . .*[1]

If anger is respected for what it is, a legitimate feeling of displeasure that responds to hurt it can become a powerful ally. If it is ignored, however, as it most often is, it will grow into a monster that must ultimately be befriended before serenity can be found.

In the following dialogue the Angry One is welcomed into consciousness and released from the closet of fear.

A Conversation with the Angry One

J.P. Anger, it has taken me a very long time to recognize your existence. I've been so afraid of you that I wanted to make believe that I was the only person alive who never got angry. I wanted to be always charitable and compassionate. Because of my fear of you, Anger, I have locked you away. I'm sorry. Would you come out into the light to talk with me now?

ANGER No, you stupid fool! When was the last time you cared? You don't give a damn about how I feel. I've been around for a long time without any recognition whatsoever. When I've come out, no thanks to you, all you do is feel apologetic. To hell with you and all your pious Christian nonsense. You just go about your business. I'll take care of myself. I always have.

J.P. But I must see you, Anger. I cannot go on without knowing what you look like and what you feel. You're absolutely right. I've ignored you and because of that you have turned very ugly. When you burst out without permission, you hurt others terribly. You can be so very cold and irritable when you take over the inner family. I can't let you go on this way. No matter what the cost, I must come face to face with you.

ANGER Oh, you sound so brave now. Why weren't you brave enough to look at me, so many years ago, before I became so ugly. It would have been so much easier to become friends when we were young. I don't think it's possible now. . .and anyway, I'm rather set in my ways. When I want to make myself known, I can do it without assistance from you. I may not be able to yell very often—you still have a tight hold on me there—but I can ignore or stare coldly at people, manipulate and hurt others, and keep you up all night with my angry thoughts. I have my ways, so don't bother playing at friendship. You don't give a damn.

J.P. Look, Angry One, I didn't know. I was taught that you were bad. I was told to stay away from you and never let you out. I almost completely forgot you existed. If you didn't remind me every now and then that you were alive and well and growing because of my fear of you, I still wouldn't pay much attention.

ANGER And with these kind words you want me to show myself. You want me to be sweet, gentle, and charitable after being ignored for years. No, I won't have it! I'll have my way or none at all. I'll take control when I want and for any reason I want. I can overcome almost every other inner family member. No one can stand in my way.

J.P. But, Anger, I don't want to stand in your way. I just want to meet you and come to know who you are and where you've come from. I don't want to dominate or master you. I just want to learn your ways and live with you. You don't have to be a monster or demon, if we can talk it out. Perhaps if we just sit down and talk for a while to find out what irritates you, we could work out an arrangement.

ANGER So you want to negotiate terms for my surrender! Not on your life.

J.P. Not surrender, but perhaps an alliance, an agreement. I don't want to get rid of you. Since you'll always be with me, I'd rather understand you. Why, do you think I want to kill you or make you a slave?

ANGER Look, I've been around for a long time. I was born with you. I'm one of your most valuable emotions. I protect you when threatened and defend you from hurt. Without me, you couldn't survive physically, emotionally, or even spiritually. I keep you from being smothered in a world where hatred can kill. I motivate you to love when justice has been harmed or people oppressed. You and your ignorant world turn me into a demon when all you want is gentle, pure, Christian comfort. I was your friend long before your fear made an enemy of me.

J.P. I'd like to know more of you, Anger. I'd like to meet you on equal ground, but you often take control at the most inappropriate moments, and then I just don't know what to do, except feel guilty and even more angry at myself for letting you rule.

ANGER OK, I get it. You want to make a deal, right? Maybe that's enough for today. If you pay a bit more attention to the fact that I am here within you and that I have rights, then perhaps I'll be a bit more selective about my aggressive behavior. How's that?

J.P. Sounds like a start anyway. I'd like to see what you look like, though. Could you just step out of the shadow of the closet a bit more so I can see you?

ANGER No, not just yet. You're not ready to see how ugly you've made me. If I notice a more accepting attitude in the future, perhaps I'll show myself. Perhaps by then I won't look so scarred.

Transforming Aggressive Energy

Befriending your anger is a liberating process. If you have ignored, buried, or repressed powerful angry feelings, they have become a foe you will one day have to reckon with in crisis. But if you are able to

name your angry feelings
name the cause or object of your anger
purify your motives
uncover hidden anger
express your anger appropriately and positively

then there is the possibility of inner serenity. As an enemy, aggressive and negative energy can cause the greatest inner family conflict and pain. Pogo's cliché, "We have met the enemy and it is us" is not quite true. I am not the enemy nor are my assertive or aggressive feelings; rather, I make these passions the enemy when I do not face them for what they are. If you do not let anger out and face it, your anger will take it out on you. The transformation of aggressive, negative energy can take place, however, if you work at befriending the Angry One.

The Guilty One

Guilt is the uncomfortable feeling or sense you have when you believe you have done something wrong or not done something you know to be right, when you blame yourself for having said something or not said something when appropriately called for, or when you have gone against your developed sense of moral responsibility or conscience. The problem with guilt, however, is that it can be both good and bad. There is such a thing as good and healthy guilt as well as inappropriate and destructive guilt. In this section we shall meet and talk with the unhealthy Guilty One, saving a conversation with the Responsible One for later.

Guilt arises when you feel you have done something wrong, but if you measure yourself against an unrealistic and superhuman ideal, then your guilt will be neurotically divisive. How you evaluate the wrong done will determine to a large extent the guilt you feel. It has been said of late that more and more people are losing the sense of conscience. Some say, "Nothing is a sin any more; then why feel guilty?" If you subscribe to the notion that there are no standards of right or wrong except those that make you feel good or bad, then your conscience and sense of responsibility are certainly underdeveloped. My experience is quite the opposite: of the people I have met and counselled, by far the larger percentage are among those who struggle with unhealthy and neurotic guilt.

Most people suffer far more from harsh self-judgment than do those who fail to judge themselves at all. One very clear characteristic of the inner Guilty One and fault-finder is that this family member feels quite inferior. Low self-esteem is the basis of unhealthy guilt. Such self-loathing drives the individual to please others whenever possible in order to find some sense of value and worth. Teenagers can often be ruled by the demon of inappropriate guilt as they constantly compare themselves to the perceived desires of their parents or the pressures of their peers. If teenagers expect to measure up to every ideal set by their parents while at the same time being acceptable to their peers, they have a big shock in store. Such self-expectations are both unreasonable and destructive.

But teens are not the only ones afflicted with the need to please everyone. From the homemaker to the corporate executive, the Guilty One finds its victim. Feelings of inferiority can drive anyone to judge themselves so harshly that they become possessed by unhealthy guilt; they become guilt-ridden.

You may not be able to describe what the voice of

guilt sounds like or remember what it said, but its great voice has more than likely spoken to you in the recent past. Let us open the closet door of the unconscious to meet the Guilty One, or perhaps more descriptively, the Fault-finder.

A Conversation with the Guilty One

J.P. Guilty One, I know you're there just below the surface of consciousness, just behind the closet door. Would you please step out so that I can talk with you for a moment?

GUILT Why would you want to talk with me? Have I done something wrong? You won't hurt me, will you? I'm very weak these days. I can only handle so much blame. If I come out and you accuse me of something, I'll surely crumble.

J.P. No, Guilty One, I won't condemn you or convict you of some wrongdoing. I'm not here to damn you. You do that well enough for the whole family. I just want to talk with you for a moment, perhaps to find out why you feel so guilty, and perhaps to show you some compassion. Please step out into the light so we can talk.

(The Guilty One, after a moment's further hesitation, finally inches around the edge of the door. With large wrinkles and tired eyes, the face is the first thing noticed. It looks as though the Guilty One could not be more than ten or twelve years old, but the weight of liability has bent the shoulders and grayed the thinning hair. The Guilty One stands in the light by the door to the unconscious with eyes lowered and head in shame. It is sad to see such a burdened creature.)

J.P. Why are you ladened with guilt, my friend? Who did this to you?

GUILT I don't know. I only know that I have to carry the responsibility of all failures. Every indiscretion of speech, every transgression of the law, real or imagined, every error, offense, crime, and sin belong to me. I'm here within you to carry the guilt for all our family members. When the Angry One loses control, I feel the shame; when you're afraid to take a risk, I'm liable; when you're insensitive or despairing, I carry the blame. I don't pile guilt upon my own shoulders; I only take what I'm given. It's you who measure out my obligation with your high standards and demanding expectations.

J.P But I never meant to victimize you, one of my very own inner family members. How have I inflicted you with expectations so heavy that they've burdened your shoulders so? Why won't you even look at me, Guilty One? What have I done to make you feel such pain?

GUILT What you've done is hold such high ideals that no one could possibly measure up to them. You want to be the best, the most successful, the greatest, the most compassionate, the one who never fails or makes a mistake. You're always trying to improve yourself because you're convinced that you're just not good enough, and I'm made to carry your lack of self-acceptance, your feelings of inferiority. Why you've built an idol you can't possibly measure up to is beyond me. Perhaps it's your warped sense of perfection that makes you heap guilt and blame on me. All I know is that if you don't break the idols you constantly compare yourself to, you'll only inflict me further. I tell you I can't take much more of this inappropriate and unrealistic blame. Without forgiveness and self-acceptance, I'll break apart, and if I do I'll take you with me.

J.P. Now calm down, Guilty One; it can't be that bad! I'm getting better at evaluating my real faults. I'm not as harsh on myself as I once was. As I get older and wiser, I've become more flexible in my self-assessment, more compassionate and forgiving toward my offenses. But I can't be, without some responsibility and ideals.

GUILT I don't want you to be without genuine and true ideals. It's the idols I can't measure up to. Ideals are one thing, values and goals to be sought through life, but you build idols when you think you should be the picture of perfection. Give me a break, won't you? Perfection is unattainable without a lot of forgiveness, love, and compassion. Why do you spend so much time striving to be more than you are? I think you'd be a lot happier, and I'd be a lot less burdened, if you'd spend some time looking at how far love has brought you and how good you are, as you are, rather than constantly looking at how high you have to climb to be perfect. If you could let go of just one false expectation, I'd be a lot lighter to carry.

J.P. I understand, Guilty One. I'll keep you in mind a little more clearly now as I pass judgment upon myself. Now that I've spoken with you and seen the load you carry, I'll be more realistic about taking on unnecessary blame. I'm sorry for having burdened you so. Thanks for coming out and showing yourself.

GUILT Be careful. You're starting to feel guilty for feeling guilty. We don't want that now, do we?

Confronting Unhealthy Guilt

When you feel unworthy or when you judge yourself too harshly, it is the voice of unhealthy guilt ruling your inner family. The voice of guilt speaks in a variety of tones and with different messages. At times our guilt speaks a language of harshness, condemning our conscious egos with negative words. Such abusive guilt is not only unhealthy but neurotically self-defeating. Perhaps you have heard some of the Guilty One's abuse:

"You did it again and everyone saw you do it."

"You really blew it this time."

"You have made a terrible mistake and you'll never be forgiven."

"That's a sin and you'll have to pay."

"God is watching your every move; don't make a mistake."

"It's your fault, your fault, your fault."

Unhealthy guilt is a dictator that subordinates and oppresses both your freedom and realistic personal responsibility. The more you identify who you are with how guilty you feel, for real or imagined wrongs, the more neurotic and divided you will become. Unhealthy guilt can make you emotionally ill.

The only way to deal with neurotic guilt is to confront it with reality, to evaluate where your true responsibility lies. Guidance may be needed to objectively discern realistic faults or errors, especially when the Guilty One has ruled for too long a time.

Here are some of the feelings or behavior patterns of those tyrannized by the Guilty One. If you find in these a picture of yourself, then you are more than likely over-identifying who you are with how guilty you feel.

• You need to be perfect, without fault or failure.

• You keep believing that there is something wrong with you, even when told differently by someone who loves you. Despite the love you receive, you feel unworthy, flawed, and unlovable.

• You consistently expect, and set yourself up for, failure in work and relationships.

• You take on obligations, tasks, and responsibilities that are not your own.

• You believe that when you enjoy life too much you must be punished, so you perhaps punish yourself by overworking, excessive eating and drinking, or drugs.

The Guilty One will never be defeated by logic or rational evaluation, but it can be healed through the power of forgiveness. By recognizing and befriending your inner Guilty One, you take the first steps toward releasing yourself from its control.

Once in a fervent passion, I cried with desperate grief: "O Lord, my soul is black with guilt. Of sinners I am chief." Then came my Guardian Angel who whispered from behind, "Vanity, my little one. You're nothing of the kind" (Anonymous).

The Addicted One

In varying degrees, every human being is an addict. Whatever you are hooked on—a feeling, a thought, an image of yourself, a person, a habit-forming chemical, a fantasy—you are to some extent conditioned. Not everything is based on free choice. The physiological and instinctual biological needs to eat and sleep, for example, are necessary addictions for the sake of life itself. You may, of course, be able to choose the amount you eat or the time you sleep, but eventually the basic need for biological life will take over for self-preservation.

The unhealthy Addicted One, however, is that part of ourselves that is so fearful of reality that escape is its only answer. Another name for the Addict is the Escapist. It is that desire we have to give ourselves over to whatever we feel will give us comfort, or pleasure. The Addict surrenders the power of choice to an idea or substance, a feeling or person, in order to find an easy escape from reality, rather than a way to deeper truth.

Addicts are not only hooked on drugs, alcohol, tobacco, or food. These are perhaps the more obvious things one can cling to as a means of coping with stress. Addictions begin in the emotional need to run from any reality that hurts, but the idea, feeling, or substance we use to escape reality is merely part of the problem. Ironically addictions grow as you compulsively attempt to escape.

For some time I have wanted to gather together a unique group of people: one member from Alcoholics Anonymous, Alanon, Alateen, Over-Eaters Anonymous, Gamblers Anonymous, Emotions Anonymous, Gamanon, and any other group based on the principles first established for use by Alcoholics Anonymous. Discussions and insights from such a group struggling for freedom would indeed be challenging. The first point these self-helpers would agree on would be, "What you are addicted to is not as important as admitting that you have an addiction." Recognizing and understanding the dynamics of addiction is the first step toward freedom, no matter what you are addicted to. When you can say, and believe, "I have an addiction that has taken control of my will and power of choice," then you can confront the Addict with reality.

Addictions deny and kill life. When a part of yourself, whether a feeling of inferiority or a need to escape, is given power, it will take over the whole of your life. Perhaps you are addicted to a fantasy life that helps you feel like a hero, or you are habitually wedded to a substance that will get you high enough so that the lows don't seem so low. Perhaps you are overly dependent on another person to make your decisions, rather than facing them yourself. Whatever you use as an escape from reality will ultimately tyrannize and destroy you. Serenity cannot be found in escape. Pleasure may be found in avoidance, for a brief moment, but never will real and lasting serenity be found.

A Conversation with the Addict

J.P. Addict, I'd like to talk with you. Will you step out from behind the closet door of the unconscious?

(Silence)

J.P. Excuse me, Addicted One, I know you're there. I can hear you breathing. Would you come out and speak with me?

ADDICT What is all this nonsense about talking with me? You think you can get rid of me just by recognizing that I exist. This is sheer psychological mumbo-jumbo. Don't you realize that as soon as you see me, your life will be just that much more difficult? You'll have to deal with what is, reality, rather than letting me get us high. Wouldn't you much prefer to take a little fantasy ride instead? There's an idea! Let's stop all this self-analysis and get high.

J.P. Get high on what?

ADDICT Sounds tempting doesn't it? Take your choice. Let's have a fantasy. I can make you king of anything. I'm good at dreams of power. How about some sexual stuff? I can give you a fantastic pleasure ride. You just let go and let me handle things. I'll come up with something that will take you far away. How about a little shot or two? Who cares what time it is. It's always time for a pop or snort. Let's have some fun. You're taking this freedom thing too damn far. You're getting so serious. You don't want to become a boring goody-goody, do you? I've got some goodies that will make you fly. Let's. . .

J.P. Hold on, will you? Just stop for a moment so I can think.

ADDICT You don't want to do that now, do you? The more you think, the more it will hurt. Relax. Stop all this reflection and let go. Trust me!

J.P. No! Now stop it! I'm tired of you and your manipulative ways. How could I ever have let you get so strong, so powerful, so cunning? I have come to talk with you today because I want freedom. I want back some of the power you've stolen from me.

ADDICT Wait a minute there, pal. I've never stolen power from you. I'm not a thief. Every ounce of control and power I have, you gave me. When you're afraid and don't want to deal with it, I take the fear away with a little fantasy or high. You're the one that gives me permission to do my thing because you can't cope with the stress of ordinary life. When you don't want to be responsible for your own feelings, you turn them over to me and I hide them; I distort them or bury them with pleasure. You're the one who has created me out of your own compulsive needs. I can only help you escape from life if you want me to. I don't operate on my own.

J.P. But you seem so much in control. When I least expect it, I find myself avoiding choices, hiding in fear, and making excuses. I don't want to be so compulsive, yet when I think everything is going well you show up with another game to play.

ADDICT You don't seem to get it, sucker. You want me around because I make life easy and carefree. Now you talk of freedom and how you want to make choices and face life, but when it gets tough you call on me for a little escape.

J.P. But that's just it. You don't make life carefree and easy. You make life even more difficult than it is already. The more I let you rule my inner family, the more poisoned my life becomes. There is no real peace found in you. I am not looking for escape but peace. There *is* a big difference, you know. Peace is more than living without conflict. It's knowing that even in the tough times there is the possibility of hope, that even when my days are filled with stress, I can handle it. I may be filled with fear at times, but one thing is for sure, Addicted One: you don't help me find happiness one damn bit. That's why I wanted to talk with you today. I thought perhaps you could release some of my power for choice, some of my will power. Perhaps we could make a deal.

ADDICT Well, if you insist. Right now you seem rather strong in your intent to gain some freedom. I guess I'd better let you go just a little bit to keep you happy, but when you're ready to run, give me a call. You have a great imagination. I can come up with trips you'll just love. When you feel frustrated, give me a yell. I'll be there to take you away from it all.

J.P. That's what I'm afraid of.

To what you are habitually addicted to, you give the power to dominate your life. Your addiction may not be as obvious as the Alcoholic's, but if your feelings or fantasies rule you, then you too suffer from the presence of the Addicted One. Deny your addiction and it can destroy you; recognize it and you can be set free.

The recovery of millions of alcoholics, food addicts, gamblers, and other emotionally addicted testifies to the preference of freedom over the prison of addiction. Whatever you are addicted to—pleasure, fantasy, a person, a feeling, an "ism"—the addiction can be arrested. The human tendency to escape reality may never be cured, but there is recovery for those who allow the inner Courageous One to choose.

The Fearful One

One of the most powerful and destructive of the sub-personalities, or family members, is fear. It is the foundation for many other negative reactions and the core around which the addictive personality is built. Fear is perhaps the strongest and, if unchecked, the most harmful of the inner selves. It has the power to prevent love itself, if left to its own insecurity.

Fear is neither good nor bad but rather a response to what you consider harmful, an absolutely essential emotion for self-protection against legitimate dangers. If you have been taught, however, that harm will come to you if you make a mistake or reveal your true thoughts or feelings, then of course you would in fear avoid these situations. If you have been taught, either directly or indirectly, that there is danger in making a mistake because others will think less of you, and if you do not face this fear as unrealistic, then your daily choices can be controlled by the need to hide your imperfections.

Gerald G. Jampolsky reveals how much fear has been an adversary in his life and what he has attempted to do about it:

> Most of my life I have acted as if I were a robot, responding to what other people said and did. Now I recognize that my responses are determined only by the decisions I make. I claim my freedom by exercising the power of my deci-

sion to see people and events with love instead
of fear.²

If you give over the power of your choice-making to the Fearful One, your perception of what is or what could be a threat is distorted by the blinders of insecurity. Whether fear is real, imagined, or projected is not as important as whether you let it rule you. When daily activities are controlled by fear, you are not freely choosing but are rather being driven by a force you give power to. If fear is conditioned by what you think is a threat, then it is appropriate to examine what you are most frequently afraid of. In other words, you have to find your fear's trigger; you have to recognize what threatens you most. Is it life itself, the possibilities of tomorrow, the memories of yesterday, or the unknown workings of God? Does the opinion of another threaten you so much that protective fear is your response? Or could it be that many of the things you are convinced will hurt you are only illusions? As this simple tale reveals, your response to a perceived threat can be more harmful than the imagined threat itself.

A man saw a poisonous snake and picked up a stick to beat it, but the snake he saw was really a stick and the stick he picked up was really a snake.

Let us now attempt a conversation with the Fearful One. Fear may perhaps be the most difficult inner self to coax into dialogue, so let us move gently.

A Conversation with Fear

J.P. Fear, I know you are standing just behind the closet door of the unconscious. You're always there. I can feel your presence as you tremble in the corner of my heart, tense and alone. You don't have to be alone. Would you come out so that we may talk?

(Silence)

J.P. I won't hurt you, Fear, or cause you harm. Please trust me. Trust the inner family. We wouldn't do anything to endanger you. Please step into the light.

FEAR Why should I show myself? You want to get rid of me. I just know it. For a long time you've been trying to kill me with your attempts at being strong. How do you think I feel when you take foolish risks or when you refuse to listen to my cries for safety? You say you want to be my friend, but I know better. You want to annihilate me.

J.P. I'm surprised, Fear; how very young your voice sounds. You couldn't be more than seven or eight years old. I didn't realize you were so young and fragile.

FEAR So what if I'm young. . .and I'm not fragile! I can master you any time I want. All I have to do is start a hurtful memory rolling and I've got you in my grasp. You want me to show my power. Just watch! Do you remember when you were laughed at for. . .

J.P. Now stop it, Fear! I don't want to talk about that right now. I remember how frightened I was, but that was years ago. Let's leave that memory alone for now. I want to talk with you out in the open. Come out here or I'm coming in after you.

FEAR Well, come on in. The family is waiting. Or are you afraid?

J.P. Here I come, Fear. (Behind the door of the unconscious there was such a darkness that I could not see. I closed my eyes from the blackness.) Fear, where are you? My heart is pounding with alarm. It's so dark in here.

FEAR If you'll just open your eyes, you'll be able to see me. How can you see when you have your eyes closed like that? The only light in here will be the light from your eyes, as soon as you open them, I'll release you from my grasp so that you can see.

J.P. Thank you, Fear. You had me in near panic for a moment. I can see how very strong you are, but where are you hiding?

FEAR Look over here.

J.P. (In the corner cowered a small, timid child, trembling with anticipation.) Oh Fear, my little one, don't tremble so; I won't hurt you. I've come to try and understand you. I just didn't realize how much of a child you were. How did you ever get locked up in here?

FEAR I'm here because you need me. I protect you from danger and pain. I'm not just your parents' leftover anxieties. I keep you safe and far from risk. I'm your friend.

J.P. Well that's true I suppose. . .to some extent. You certainly do keep me out of trouble at times, but you do far more than that: you keep me too safe. With your trembling, you prevent me from making decisions, or taking risks that will help me grow, or meeting people I want to know. You smother me with your protection, placing unreasonable limits around me. Your boundaries are too tight, Fear. They're ruining my opportunities for happiness. Why don't you let go of some of your protecting power so that I can make some of my own decisions?

FEAR Well, where did all this daring sense of confidence come from? You've always let me be your protector. You liked the limits I set. Since when has freedom counted more than the safety of my boundaries?

J.P. Ever since I realized that the happiness that comes from safety is boring me to death. If you don't give me some of my freedom, Fear, and let go of some of your energy, we'll all wither away.

FEAR Well, perhaps I could let go just a bit. I've been clinging to security rather tightly of late. I guess I knew this quest for freedom was getting serious. Mind you, I can't let go completely; you need some limits.

J.P. I know and I respect that. But please loosen your grip just a bit from the blanket of protection so that I can dare to make choices and take chances. It's the only way we'll grow. Oh, before I leave, Fear, could you tell me if the Worrier is around somewhere? I thought you would perhaps be hiding near the Worrier.

FEAR Yes, the Worrier and I are close. We're related you know. Without me, the Worrier can't exist. I'm not sure where the Worrier is right now, but I bet it won't be long before the Worrier will want to talk to you.

J.P. OK. Well, if you'd tell the Worrier that I'll be back in a few moments, I'd appreciate it. By the way, thanks for inviting me into the closet. You're the first to invite me in.

Freedom From Fear

Fear prevents us from making free choices based on attentive will. It is an obstacle to decisions that require faith, risk-taking, and confidence. It prevents growth. For example, the greatest obstacle for those with an emotional difficulty who need professional help is most often the fear of what others will think if they sought counselling or therapy. No one will choose freedom and health until they are tired of being sick with fear. Fear constantly attempts to undermine responsible self-direction. You have to develop an attitude of self-observation which can lead to liberation.

In varying degrees, everyone hears the same message from Fear:

"You will only be hurt."
"Better safe than sorry."
"Don't try anything new; you'll only fail."
"What is old is good; what is new is bad."
"Caution: danger ahead!"

The messages of unconscious fear are only convincing if you give them the power to motivate your actions. But if you recognize such statements as the obstacles to growth that they can be, you will experience a new freedom for choice. If you face your fears, no matter how terrifying they are, not only will energy for decision making be released, but the possibility of serenity will be that much more possible.

The Worrier

There is one more potentially destructive inner self to be confronted, the Worrier. There are, of course, as many passions turned foes as you create by over-identification, but I have chosen to dialogue with only the most dominant.

The Worrier is a friend of Fear, perhaps Fear's cousin. Worry grows strong as Fear grows more powerful. It is only when you over-identify with your feelings of fear that anxiety begins to consume your psychic energy, filling your mind, body, and heart with worries. Anxiety is a persistent, nagging tension that causes you to expect the worst.

For some, worrying is a pastime, a thing to do when all is going smoothly. Worriers, preoccupied with the possibilities of hurt, become especially adept at playing the games of "What if?" and "I can't."

To play the self-destructive game of "What if?" you must follow the neurotic rules of warped thinking. First, you must always expect the worst. Second, if someone attempts to calm you down with reasons, you should become even more anxious. Third, to become a full-fledged worrywart you must have a pessimistic perspective that sees calamity in every possibility. The psychological game of "What if?" is best played by those plagued by anxiety attacks. These recurring and sudden bursts of apprehension can possess us with the worrisome questions: "What if it happens again? What will I do?"

Habitual and frequently needless worry can haunt the most seemingly confident individuals. Business executives can be plagued by anxiety over the dreadful possibility that their business will not do well, or a mother can become vexed by the nagging worry that her child will be hurt if allowed out of her sight for the moment. When you project your greatest apprehension into the future, your confidence is overwhelmed by the demon of worry.

The second psychological game played by the Worrier is illustrated by a saying from the Christian Bible (Matthew 6:34). Jesus tells his followers,

> Enough, then, of worrying about tomorrow. Let tomorrow take care of itself. Today has troubles enough of its own.

The problem with worriers is that they are convinced, based either on hurtful experiences from the past or projections of fear into the future, that they cannot handle the troubles of today or tomorrow. Such negative expectations and fearful projections act as a barrier to creative confidence. Worriers feel so unable to cope with the anticipated threat that they become locked in the game of "I can't." They expect the worst and prepare for it by not dealing with it at all. They avoid reality by brooding over the troubles of yesterday or by fretting in the face of tomorrow's possible problems. If they allow the Worrier to linger in the mind, it will ultimately take its toll on the body through hypochondria, ulcers, high blood pressure, back problems, and many other psychosomatic complaints. In the final analysis, possession by the demon of over concern, is not a game; it can become a life-threatening obsession.

A Conversation with Worry

J.P. I'd like to speak with the Worrier now. Fear, would you introduce me to your friend, the Worrier?

FEAR I'm not sure the Worrier wants to speak with you right now. He's rather hesitant, you understand. He's not sure what will happen if he speaks with you. He's rather concerned about your motives.

J.P. That's always the concern of the Worrier; he's never sure. Well, I can't assure him that everything will go exactly his way, but I can guarantee I won't hurt him in any way. If the Worrier would just step out from behind his needless apprehension for a moment, we could talk. We can work out any problems that might arise.

WORRIER You sound so confident. Don't you realize what's about to happen? What's the matter with you? Are you blinded by your naive optimism?

J.P. I don't understand. What's about to happen that causes you to be so beset by pessimism?

WORRIER Oh, for God's sake, look at your life. Look how happy you feel, how much success you have, and how healthy you are. You have no real troubles to speak of. Doesn't all this good fortune scare you?

J.P. But why would success or health scare me?

WORRIER Isn't it obvious? Oh sure, you feel happy right now. . .but wait. What if you get sick or lose your job? What then? I just know that tragedy is right around the corner. I can feel it. Don't you know that you can't trust life when things go too well? Things can turn sour at any time.

J.P. Let's be a bit more realistic, please. You sound like you believe Murphy's Law: "If anything can go wrong, it will." I don't believe in such twisted fate. I'm not a fool and I don't take unnecessary chances. Even if something harmful did happen, we could handle it. You're so plagued by pessimistic concerns that you forget that I do have some strength, some ability to confront and deal with problems.

WORRIER Go ahead, walk confidently through life if you want. I'll continue my vigil in case of an accident.

J.P. Now wait a minute, Worrier. You do a hell of a lot more than keep vigil. You're not just some nice protector who defends me from what may hurt. You look for and search out every little risk precisely so you can avoid it. By expecting trouble, you make trouble for the whole inner family. I can't allow you to victimize me with your anxiety. You create more harm than you help me avoid. I won't let you continue your harassment by anticipating calamity at every turn or by tormenting me with negative possibilities. You're not going to have your way in the future, I can tell you that. Are you there, Worrier? Worrier?

(Silence)

J.P. Worrier, are you there?

(Silence)

FEAR I'm sorry, you scared the Worrier with your challenge. He is pouting and won't talk with you any more. He was afraid you'd hurt him and that's exactly what you did. It may be quite a while before he'll trust you again.

J.P. Well, the Worrier always seems to find more to worry about. Fear, would you tell the Worrier that there's no other way to grow but to face reality? I know it's difficult to do but we have to for sanity's sake. Tell the Worrier that in the long run it's better to face the problems of today, today, rather than hiding in tomorrow. We'll talk again, I'm sure.

John Powell, S.J. describes the way of the worrier:

> As a game, worry is an immature way to handle one's difficulties. The worrier usually gets on a treadmill, goes over the same ground again and again, getting nowhere. He repeats useless statements of his problems, rehearses alternatives without reaching any decisions and counts all the possible consequences of possible decisions again and again. The worrier would probably feel guilt for not doing anything constructive, so he does something: he worries.[3]

The alternative to trusting the present and your capacity to deal with it is anxiety. The worrier is the victim of an anxiety that continually focuses on what is over, is not yet, or what may not be at all.

More is required, though, to deal with destructive worry than to be told, "Don't worry; everything will work out." There is nothing more irritating than to be told not to feel the emotion you are practically possessed by. When you are up-tight with anxiety, letting go is not enough. In order to release the energy that would be consumed by worry, you must be honest enough to face your tendency to over-identify with pessimism. To confess your unrealistic fears and confront them.

Throughout this chapter, I have referred to the feelings of anger, guilt, fear, and worry as enemies. No emotions are born as negative voices. Rather, they become negative, enemies, when you do not respect them for what they are. When you ignore your basic human emotions, you turn them into enemies.

Your feelings are not enemies to run from or to fight with but aspects of your personality to be listened to. How you feel is a part of the unique miracle of who you are. The more you ignore how you feel, the more you empower your emotions to consume you with a force that can break you down physically, psychologically, and spiritually. When you make an emotion your enemy, you give it the power to destroy you. When you worship your emotions, you make of them idols.

Feelings are not meant merely to be followed, however, as though every emotion and passion you have is positive. It is better to befriend your feelings than to follow them blindly. It is far better to recognize the power struggle that goes on among your various selves, your emotions, and attempt to transform the negative energy of conflict into a positive energy for purpose.

Chapter Four

Lifelong Inner Friends

When looking at psychological dynamics there is a tendency to emphasize the negative. We see a preoccupation with illness rather than health, demons over allies, nightmares over dreams. Character flaws are far more intriguing than the positive inner qualities. Good news about the possibilities of emotional health, potential for creative change, and transformation of destructive psychic energy are not entertaining enough for the evening news. The struggle for serenity, the dynamic growth toward reconciliation and friendship within are not as interesting as emotional traumas, inner conflicts, and neurotic wars. No matter how much the human spirit prefers the light, there is a nagging preoccupation with the dark side of the soul.

I believe, as Norman Cousins does, that the sublime wonder and potential of the human personality are so intriguing that they are almost too much to bear:

> *Considering the number of different species on the planet, the chances of being born a human being are about one in two billion. Considering the number of sperm produced by a single mating experience, the particular sperm that resulted in you was one in several million, at least. What is most astounding of all, however,*

43

*is the absence of human awareness of the phe-
nomenal triumph over impossible odds that a
single human being represents. Human beings
have been able to comprehend everything in
the world except their uniqueness. Perhaps it
is just as well. If ever we begin to contemplate
our own composite wonder, we will lose ourselves in celebration and have time for nothing
else.[1]*

No matter how many so-called inner adversaries attack, the human spirit is strong enough to triumph. With
an attentive will, inner conflict can be reconciled. Such
healing growth does not take place by merely
"accentuating the positive," as the old song goes, but by
first recognizing the paradoxical truth that the opposite
is always true. Within each of us there seems to be passionate enemies who can overwhelm us if we give them
the power to rule, but there are also passionate friends
who have a grace-filled reservoir of power to save us
from ourselves.

Coventry Patmore observes that the difference between a sinner and a saint is not whether one has emotions and the other has no passions at all, but rather in
how each faces, copes with, disciplines, and harnesses
the passionate feelings that arise.

*The power of the soul for good is in proportion
to the strengths of its passions. Sanctity is not
the negation of passion—feeling—but its order.
Hence great saints have often been great sinners.[2]*

To the extent that you repress your negative feelings, for fear of their power to destroy, to that extent do
you also deny yourself your positive passions. It may not
be difficult to realize that within you are the most destructive of enemies. Perhaps you struggle with them so

often that they have become all too familiar. But to what degree are you able to affirm that within you are also the highest and most sublime of human qualities, your friends? Just as there are inner negative voices that wound your sense of self-esteem, so there are positive voices that affirm your integrity as an individual. It is sad that many people are so busy creating and fighting enemies within, that they never meet the passionate allies for life that also live there.

I will now introduce to you some of your lifelong friends within, lifelong because they can be overwhelmed only for a time, never defeated completely. No matter how much you have been burdened by emotional pain, the possibility of furious love, generativity, courage, hope, and responsibility is still alive. These friends are waiting behind the closet door of your unconscious, ready to break through if you will only get out of your own way.

The Furious Lover

In the history of cultural and personal growth, anger (yes, anger) has played a very important role. It can be, and often has been, a close friend of progress. The problem is that if you repress the anger that burns, you also ignore its potential for furious love. Anger can either destroy life or build life, inflict wounds or alleviate pain. Whether it is a destructive foe or a compassionate friend depends on whether it is motivated by self-centered righteousness or by empathetic understanding.

Anger motivated by a deep empathy for those who suffer misfortune, or by a desire to alleviate pain, or by a compassionate understanding of injustice and the rights of others, is certainly not a negative, aggressive foe but a positive friend. I call this self, this inner family member, the Furious Lover because it is that part of each of us that is aroused by legitimate concern.

The Furious Lover is able to commiserate with those in pain and fight for the rights of the oppressed. The Furious Lover is more interested in getting rights for another than in getting her own way. The compassionate inner self, another name for the Furious Lover, is that part of you that recognizes how deeply connected each member of the human family is. When the hurt of another becomes your hurt, the injustice against another, an injustice against you, you realize how interdependent all humans are.

The story is told that when Florence Nightingale was asked what prompted her to give her life to the service of others in difficult hospital work, she responded, "Rage." Another example of the Furious Lover in operation is found in Mother Teresa of Calcutta. When asked why she worked with the poorest of the poor, the beggars and sick of the streets, she is supposed to have said, "It is not for success but for faith." When you care only for yourself, anger is usually a negative feeling that desires domination over others. When you care for the rights of others, the dignity of your brothers and sisters, and for the possibility of creative change, anger becomes a compassionate friend that will fight injustice with non-violence, while seeking the valued reality of peace. When power over, insensitivity to, and ignorance of, the rights and needs of others is the motivating force behind your anger, you are possessed by a demon power. When anger is motivated by power for, tenderness toward, and awareness of the needs of others, you are guided by the spirit of compassion.

The Furious Lover, however, does not merely love with a superficial emotional care that does not challenge. Love can be, and often must be, tough if it is to be truly compassionate. Self-help groups such as Alcoholics Anonymous, Tough Love, and many others understand that love must at times challenge the comfortable. Look at the Furious Love of Jesus the Christ. His constant love did not merely soothe the afflicted and oppressed but also challenged the complacent. In the story of the money changers in the Temple, Christ's anger is an example of Furious Love (Mark 11:15-17).

> So (Jesus and his disciples) reached Jerusalem and he went into the temple and began driving out those who were selling and buying there; he upset the tables and the chairs of those who were selling pigeons. Nor would he allow anyone to carry anything through the temple. And he taught them and said, "Does not scripture say: 'My house will be called a house of prayer for all peoples'? But you have turned it into a robbers den."

Such rage was meant to shock those in the status quo. Christ's anger was an anger of love, expressed at times to awaken the materialistic and indifferent. Furious Love confronts with reality rather than pacifies with illusions. It is aggressive anger befriended, and transformed from a destructive power that steals from life to a constructive force for life. If your angry feelings are inflamed by the need for power, the heat of your anger will scorch your soul and the lives of others. But if your anger is ignited by the burning desire of compassionate understanding, justice will be your goal. Let us now meet the Furious Lover who lives within each of us.

Conversation with the Furious Lover

J.P. I'm not exactly sure how I should address you, Furious Lover; you show yourself in so many ways. At one moment you are compassionate, at another, merciful, yet in other situations you show yourself through rage. I know you're not a do-gooder or self-righteous one, but I am a bit confused. Your love has so many faces.

FURIOUS LOVER First of all, let me thank you for the opportunity to speak with you. You are so often trapped by negative feelings of bitterness that you forget that I also live in you. What you call me does not matter so much as the fact that you recognize my presence. "Furious Lover" is an appropriate name during these times when indifference and arrogance rule. But feel free to call me what you choose.

J.P. Why do you care so much, my friend? Already you've mentioned the power struggles around us. Why do you feel such anguish in the face of human cruelty and injustice?

FURIOUS LOVER I care because hurt is not foreign to our family. I have felt pain, experienced misfortune, had my rights violated and been abused by the fears of others; I understand what it is to suffer. The only way I can live with my suffering is to help others cope with theirs. The only way I can be free is to help others find freedom. This may sound a bit selfish, as though I love only to be loved, but that is not the case. I care because I am so thankful for the compassion shown to me. It has set me free. I have compassion for others because it has been shared with me. When you experience love, you want to love; when you are understood, you desire to understand; when you have been freed, you are driven to free others. I do not give love in order to receive, but that is what happens. I can't deny it.

J.P. You sound so wise. I thought I'd meet someone burning up with anger. How are you so calm when you see misery abound? Why aren't you yelling at me to do more for others, to pay more attention to you, to stop giving in to my petty concerns? I must admit, I was a bit afraid of meeting you; I thought your love would be difficult to handle.

FURIOUS LOVER That's one of your problems. You want to manipulate love so that it won't threaten your precious little world. I hurt with love because I see rights invaded, freedom ignored, and hope destroyed by arrogant power-hungry monsters. Did you know that a gun is sold in the United States every thirteen seconds? In South Africa, thousands starve because of apartheid, while the upper class purchases new cars. In some parts of Northern Ireland, children learn to shoot a gun before they are old enough to learn how to make love. In Iran, young men, children really, look forward to death in battle as a way to heaven. Did you know that every twenty seconds someone kills another person? Love sees all this and more. Love hurts like hell but, if it is true and honest love, it won't be consumed by flames of bitterness. It will, instead, be inflamed with the desire to change the world.

J.P. But I can't change the world. How can you expect me to deal with all the violence and hatred? I can't take upon myself all the suffering inflicted on others. That's too much to expect.

FURIOUS LOVER First of all, you can do a great deal more than you think. You may not want to care so much that it hurts, but there's a real difference between saying, "I can't love" and "I won't love." I don't expect you to change the world, but I do expect you to want the world to change for the better. I not only want, I demand, that you let go of your indifference by first changing yourself. I beg you, call on my compassion to love more often than you allow fear to overpower you. Choose to serve rather than expecting to be served all the time. Let my voice of tenderness be heard more than the whining voice of fear. I guarantee, the only ones who know true serenity are those who serve rather than are served; those who share rather than take; those who love rather than victimize. There is no serenity without struggle, no love without furious anger.

J.P. Thank you, Furious Lover. I'll talk with you again soon. Perhaps you could stay closer to my awareness so that I can find you more easily than I do the Fearful One. Would you do that?

FURIOUS LOVER Where I sit among your selves in

the inner family is up to you. You're the only one who can move me closer to conscious realization.

The Furious Lover knows what rights belong to each person and loves enough to fight for them. The Furious Lover within Norman Cousins expresses the human rights of each human being in this way:

Certain rights are acquired by a human being just in the act of being born:

> *The right to grow and to meet one's individual potentialities.*
>
> *The right to appraise and apply one's abilities, consistent with the rights of others.*
>
> *The right to one's thoughts. The right to nourish and voice them.*
>
> *The right to make mistakes, whether of thought or deed, without fear of unjust punishment.*
>
> *The right to hope.*
>
> *The right to justice, whether the claim is against a person, an aggregation, or government itself.*
>
> *The right to contemplate human destiny and the mysteries of existence, or to detach oneself altogether from these pursuits.*
>
> *The right to hold grievances against one's society and to make them known to others.*
>
> *The right to make a better life for our young.*[3]

I would add one more right to the above list. The right to feel Furious Love and to act upon it with non-violent acts of justice.

The Responsible One

During my early years in the seminary a wise teacher frequently told me, "I was responsible for what I saw,

and any personal knowledge I gained was for the purpose of greater responsibility." I resisted this basic moral tenet for quite some time, believing, as so many did
in the 1960s, that autonomy was the ultimate goal of life.
Like so many others trapped in the egocentric desire for
self-sufficiency and unlimited independence, I too be-
lieved that responsibility was for the compliant and passive members of society who were not strong or brave
enough to rise above the status quo. Words like discipline, duty, obligation and commitment were of less importance than freedom, self-realization, self-
actualization, ι nd self-development.

It was not until I began to face my own irresponsi-
ble desire for autonomy, "doing my own thing," that I
realized how related freedom and responsibility are. As
Marilyn Ferguson writes:

> The discovery of freedom, for instance, means
> little if we are not empowered to act, to be free
> for something, not just from something. As fear
> falls away, we are less afraid of power's Siamese
> twin, responsibility.[4]

The more freedom you achieve from the self-made
demons of anger, fear, guilt, and worry, the more energy
you have to give and the more responsible you are for
what you see. Self-knowledge liberates so that you can
learn to cooperate with what is beyond you, both in society and in the transcendent. The more you breathe inner
freedom, the more you must conspire with others to
achieve the greatest good for all.

Responsibility is not merely being in agreement
with the values and goals set by others, and freedom
does not mean autonomously doing what you want to do.
Freedom and responsibility are as linked to one another
as you are to living in community. You are a social creature, one among many, struggling toward serenity. To
the extent that you seek to live in your own world and

make your own moral laws, to that extent are you being unfaithful to your deeper self, which desires participation in and cooperation with something beyond. That "something beyond" may be the good of society or the will of God. Whatever it is, it calls you to choose responsibility, surrendering mere self-sufficiency. The more you work at personal growth, whether through spiritual direction, prayer, therapy, counselling, or self-actualization groups, the more aware you become of your power to choose. The more you see clearly the dynamics of your inner world, coming to know well your many negative selves, the freer you become to live with and respond to the needs of others. Marilyn Ferguson recognizes this point clearly:

> A sobering discovery—not guilt, not duty, but responsibility in the naked sense of its Latin roots—the act of giving back, responding. We can choose our mode of participation in the world, our response to life. We can be angry, gracious, humorous, empathetic, paranoid. Once we become aware of our habitual responses, we see the ways in which we have perpetrated many of our own tribulations.[5]

For those whose goals are freedom *from* rather than freedom *for* and power *over* rather than power *for*, responsibility is a negative concept. Since they are blinded by their own needs, they cannot see their debt and obligation to the human family and to God. Responsibility is for those who are free enough to choose it and daring enough to answer the call of the small voice of conscience that says, "You are free to choose the good."

Conversation with the Conscience

J.P. I'm not quite sure I really want to speak with you, Conscience. Whenever I hear your voice, it's usually to bother me with guilt.

CONSCIENCE That's not true at all. You just listen more consciously when I tell you that you have done something wrong. Don't you think I do more than just cause you to feel guilty when you have sinned? I'm far more than the voice of guilt.

J P. It seems the only time I notice you is when you chastise me and correct me for some wrong I did. I didn't realize you did more than pass judgment on what is good or bad.

CONSCIENCE Well, of course, the evaluation of what is good and healthy and of what is evil and destructive is my primary concern, but I'd prefer to see myself in a broader fashion. I like to think of myself as described by a Hindu sage: "the invisible God that dwells within." I'm not just reflective knowledge, or guilt consciousness, or a standard of morality; I'm far more than a voice for reason. I'm the attitude and virtue of charity that was planted in you from birth. I am the ultimate purpose that calls you to be all that you are and to act accordingly. I'm not merely some blind instinct that forces you to do good, but a motivator for growth. Without me, you wouldn't be healthy, happy, or holy. You need me to guide you on the path toward balance.

J.P. You make yourself sound like a god.

CONSCIENCE No, I don't, but it's strange that you say that, because some people would prefer to think of me as a demon, as a super-ego intent upon imprisoning you with neurotic anxieties and moral hang-ups. I'm much closer to being the oracle of the eternal truth than I am to being the damning voice of guilt-ridden parents and teachers. I have a great deal more to do with love than with guilt. I speak as the voice of healthy guilt and responsibility only when you go against what is loving and just, life-giving and prudent. My primary task is not to judge you harshly but to speak the truth with love. I know that truth sometimes challenges you and perhaps at times even hurts you, but I assure you it is always spoken with love.

J.P. Yes, but who decides what is loving or just, life-giving or prudent? That's where you are most confusing, Conscience. Who tells you what's right or wrong?

CONSCIENCE Well now, that's not easy to explain. To understand takes a bit of faith. You see, I am formed by a combination of emotional, spiritual, and intellectual growth. I dwell in you because God dwells in you. Without God, the principles and values of mercy and love would be mere shadows. I'm the super-consciousness that God is within you. I remind you of the good your life is created for, the love that can guide you and the justice you should share with others. This is a large undertaking and you have to work to help me succeed. You have to accept the responsibility to think about your life, its purpose, its goals, its reason for being. You have to choose to love yourself, your neighbor, your God. No one can do this for you. If you care enough for your own growth, you'll be guided by information and reflection rather than by momentary feelings. I'm an attitude that grows strong and healthy by attention and work. God created you as an image of the divine; therefore, you're disposed toward what is good. But a person must still form and inform his or her own conscience. No one else can do it.

J.P. I guess this means that I can't decide on my own what is right or wrong. Is that right?

CONSCIENCE Well, they say that in the final analysis I'm the ultimate decision maker for your actions, even if I am wrong occasionally. However, making your decisions without the benefit of the wisdom of others and the grace of God would be foolish indeed. I can see you have a great deal more to learn about making good, holy, and healthy decisions. That's OK. I have your lifetime and beyond to grow. You have come a long way in learning to judge justly, love faithfully, and choose prudently, but we'll continue to work together and grow.

J.P. Thanks for speaking with me, Conscience. I appreciate your guidance.

CONSCIENCE Oh, one more thing. I'll still bother you when your refuse to be all that you are and can become.

J.P. I understand.

Courageous One

In the final analysis, as Booker T. Washington reminded us, "Success is measured not so much by the positions that one has reached in life as by the obstacles which one has overcome while trying to succeed." Every person has the possibility of succeeding on the personal, social, and spiritual level, but only if the challenge is first taken up. Confidence and valor are gifts of the highest power; they live within but extend beyond the self. Courage is an endowment, a lifelong friend that will strengthen you when overwhelmed by fear, lift you up when bent low with worry, and transform your bitterness into creative energy.

Courage is not a gift bestowed on some but withheld from others. No one is without it to meet life's challenges. It is just that some never bother, or are too afraid, to stake their life on their own capacity for courage. Its essence lies in faith, the conviction and quality of spirit that enables you to see opportunity in every difficulty.

Richard Cushing, a Catholic prelate and a man of some daring, is supposed to have said, when lamenting the lack of courage:

"A great deal of talent is lost in the world for want of a little courage. Every day sends to their graves obscure men and women whom timidity prevented from making a first effort; who, if they could have been induced to begin, would in all probability have gone great lengths in the career of fame. The fact is that to do anything in the world worth doing we must not stand back shivering and thinking of the cold and danger but jump in and scramble through as well as we can."

Cushing does not assert that fame is the highest human achievement, but rather encourages the use of every talent and quality to find happiness. No happiness can be found without releasing every latent ability for the search.

If all you do is drift through life, waiting for "it" to give you what you want, if all you do is dodge the difficulties that come your way, what sense of fulfillment will you have? If human beings must be judged, then let them best be judged as Norman Cousins suggests:

> . . .by the challenges they define for themselves. So far, they have attached more importance to the challenge of adventure than to the challenge of compassion, more importance to the challenge of technological grandeur than to the challenge of human growth, more importance to the challenge of war than to the challenge of peace, more importance to the challenge of productivity than to the challenge of perspective, more importance to the challenge of the scientific intelligence than to the human spirit.[6]

There is no more difficult challenge, or more daring adventure to undertake, than trying to live with your many selves with serenity and purposefulness. The inner adventure demands far more conviction of purpose and firmness of faith than does the adventure toward fame, wealth, or power. To face the warring, competitive inner selves, those obstacles that stunt growth, requires a courage that can only be found in faith.

If you want to find courage, look to those whose faith in themselves and in God is strong. Speak with those who are physically handicapped but who only see themselves as more physically challenged. Speak with those who courageously live one day at a time because everyone has courage enough to get through just one day. Speak to those who know the inner journey of the soul, who have met with courage the inner demons of fear, anger, guilt, and worry. Speak with those who know failure yet have not been overcome, know addiction and yet are recovering, or know success but are wise enough to realize they did not do it alone.

Courage can be found by anyone who takes the risk that the deeper truth is always there and can be "proven" by an act of faith. The courageous person realizes that there are reservoirs of strength and resources of ability within, waiting for the freedom to be creative. The great challenge is not in making much money or in building a better nuclear arsenal than the enemy's. The real challenge is whether you can find the resources and courage to live with your selves. If you can do that, you can live with anyone, any challenge.

Conversation with Courage

COURAGE I'm ready. Let's talk. I've been at your side ever since you decided to face your many selves. You didn't think you were able to dialogue with your fears, guilts, angers, worries, and addictions without my help, did you? I've been here all along, encouraging and nudging you toward freedom. I must say you've done quite well.

J.P. Thank you, Courage. It's good to know that I'm not alone. However, I have a question. Where did you come from and why is it that I sometimes let depression, low self-esteem, and fear control me? If everything is possible, why isn't it possible to keep you active and alive all the time? That way, I would never feel fear again.

COURAGE Well, first of all, that's three questions, not one. Let's take them one at a time. Where did I come from? Well, I came to you first as a gift of love. Some call my source God, others call it the higher power, but in either case I am a gift of love. But a gift is valuable only if it is well received. As you were nurtured by those who loved you, so was I nurtured. As others cared for you I became strong. I didn't just pop into existence. I grew in strength as you learned to be faithful to your deeper and eternal selves.

J.P. I know I owe a great debt to others, especially those who have taught me how to love my selves, but why do you show yourself only when things get rough, when I have a problem? Why aren't you with me all the time?

COURAGE OK, a little patience, please. It's strange that you ask why I'm strong one moment while seeming to hide the next. I have never hidden myself from you. I'm here all the time, trying my level best to get your attention. The only times I'm not strong is when you focus your attention on concern and fear. I'm always ready to help you do the impossible. . .or at least the improbable. I'm always prepared to risk comfort to meet challenges. All you have to do is get your fear out of my way.

J.P. You sound so daring. How do I know you won't go too far and take too many chances? I don't want to be a hero. I just want to feel a sense of confidence.

COURAGE Look, I'm not the Great Achiever who wants the glory of great accomplishments, nor am I the Imprudent Adventurer who will lead you into more danger than you can handle. I'm the honest Courage built on faith, prudence, and wisdom. At times, I may have to rise up like a warrior to help you defeat the enemies of fear and anger, but that's rare. I try to be as consistent as I can in my confidence, within the boundaries of what you can handle. I won't force you to face challenges you're not ready for, but I'll always ask you to do a bit more than your fears will allow.

J.P. Now that I think about it, Courage, you've been around for quiet a while. I can remember when we dared to take the risk of falling in love, and when I have been in a real emotional crisis, you were there.

COURAGE That's true, I was. Not only was I there, I also grew stronger with each difficulty you faced. With each leap of faith in yourself, I became healthier and more a part of you.

J.P. I can see now why you call yourself a gift. With each recollection of a problem solved, a crisis faced, or an obstacle overcome, I can also recall that another person encouraged me and held me up when I was weak, who had faith in me when my faith was lost. I have truly leaned on the courage and strength of others.

COURAGE That's right! There are some wonderful people in your life who have given you their strength when you needed it. Without those people, you wouldn't be so strong.

J.P. I appreciate you speaking with me, Courage. Why not stay around a bit longer to continue this conversation?

COURAGE I'm not going to leave you now. I'll be around when you want me.

The Hopeful One

The longing for something better—fuller, deeper, higher, more fulfilling—is the foundation of hope. As faith grows in what is possible, hope grows in expectation. The patient, realistic yearning for the good promised fills us with hope. Provable facts are not enough to bring forth hope, nor can logic convince you that tomorrow will be better than today. Hope cannot be built on the insecure ground of logical analysis. As Norman Cousins points out:

> Hope may be fortified by experience but that is
> not where it begins. It begins in the certainty

*that things can be done that have never been
done before. This is the ultimate reality and it
defines the uniqueness of the human mind.[7]*

Hope is built not on what is, as much as on what is
expected. Keeping your eye on the promised goal of
health, happiness, and holiness is more important than
trying to figure out every step along the way. As Dag
Hammarskjold, the former Secretary General of the
United Nations, recommends:

*Never look down to test the ground before tak-
ing your next step: only he who keeps his eye
fixed on the far horizon will find his right
road.[8]*

Hope provides us with the energy to deal with enor-
mous tragedies and monstrous demons because tomorrow can be better. Hope grows as you keep your eyes
fixed on the imagined goal. It does not measure how difficult the road will be, how painful the task, how much
work will be demanded. It knows only that the promise
of fulfillment will be realized by those with faith strong
enough to keep on trying.

Some have said that the greatest evil one can inflict
on others is to force them into an existence without options, a ghetto of oppressive injustice. But even in the
midst of such evil, hope can live. The only one capable of
killing hope is oneself. Suffering, loneliness, imprison-
ment, loss, injustice, and cruelty cannot overcome hope
without the permission of despair. To give in to despair
is to still the only voice that can save you from the madness of provable facts and logical assessment: hope

What cannot be imagined is the only real barrier to
hope. If you can imagine salvation, you can prepare for it;
if you can imagine personal fulfillment, you can work for
it; if you can imagine serenity, you can find it. Belief is
the motive of hope. No matter how high the mountain

you hope to climb, how evil the affliction you confront, faith makes its achievement reachable. If you pay more attention to the goal desired rather than the difficult task of achieving it, you will ultimately discover that the goal is not as high as you first thought. If you listen to the voice of worry, you will never climb the mountain.

Never measure the height of a mountain, until you have reached the top. Then you will see how low it is.[9]

When you are setting goals or making decisions, you are supposed to "act reasonably," "expect little so that when you get more it will be a surprise," or "always keep both feet on the ground." But hope demands that you live on the edge of failure, letting go of what is merely reasonable to expect. A person guided by the voice of hope

Values times of darkness as much as periods of joy and enlightenment.

Emphasizes the importance of using obstacles as steps to growth rather than promising their complete disappearance.

Opts more for doubting and risking rather than guaranteed safety or ecstasy.

Prefers the creativity of confusion to the deceptive "clarity" of ready-made answers.

Reminds us of effort as much as effortlessness.

Acknowledges the immense variability of human beings and therefore promises no standard results.

Praises the unexpected event that shatters in one moment our model of how it should be.[10]

You will notice in the following dialogue with Hope that its vocabulary is somewhat limited. Hope finds it very difficult to say such words as: but, should, limitation, can't, if only, doubt, impossible, it's not worth it, or don't bother. These are the words of fear and insecurity, not the words of Hope.

Conversation with Hope

J.P. I don't know why you haven't been overcome, Hope, why you still cling to your enthusiasm, your optimistic stance. When I look at the world and within, all I can see at times are your enemies. How do you survive, Hope, in the face of so much pain?

HOPE I survive because there is a future. Without the possibility of tomorrow, I would not be. When the world was set in motion by the divine spark of love, I was locked together with promise, forever. No one can defeat me as long as there's a tomorrow. Neither fear, anger, pessimism, or guilt can touch me as long as there is the potential for another day. In fact, not even death can destroy me, if there's faith in the eternal tomorrow. I must say, people have surely tried to bury me with despair, but as always, I return.

J.P. There have been times when I felt lost in hopelessness and overcome by grief, but yet you have been there at the most crucial moments. When I thought I could bear no more and that all my options and possibilities were closed, or when my imagination was swamped with sadness, you would rise with just a glimmer of life-giving promise.

HOPE That's because I live beyond you as well as deep within. I am, by the grace of God and the courage of humanity, an energy of the cosmos. I'm not merely a feeling that can come or go. I'm as present as tomorrow, as real as your imagination and as close as your dreams. I live within the creative spirit of humanity and flow from the source of all that is. To destroy me would be to destroy your deepest self. Only those who are sick with the evil of despair can lose sight of me, and even to these I continue to hold out promise.

J.P. You're so good to talk to. With you, I feel a sense of calm, a serenity that so often seems to escape me. I feel enthused, as though there is nothing we can't do together.

HOPE I speak in many tones. When you're most disturbed by your own inner thoughts of limitation, I can reassure you with positive encouragement. When you wallow in comfortable and passive carelessness, I can be a voice of challenge that will stir you to rise from your sleep and move on. You don't realize how often I speak to you and how often you lean on me for meaning and purpose.

J.P. You are a friend that I have denied, yet a friend indeed, for you have not walked away. I'm most thankful for your presence.

HOPE There, you have hit it right on the head. How marvelous! Without even a hint, you found why hope is possible. As long as you can be thankful for your life, you will find me. Hope flows from gratefulness for yesterday, even if you lived it poorly, thankfulness for today, despite it difficulties, and appreciation for tomorrow, with all its untapped possibilities. In every word of thanks, you speak a word of hope.

J.P. Bless you, Hope, for your consistency as a lifelong friend.

In the face of all known statistics that rank the growth of human cruelty flies the reality of hope. Hope lived in the Nazi prison camps, despite the abominations. It lives in South Africa amidst bigotry and oppression. It lives in a hospital ward as children cry, and in a society that will fight for the rights of those born and unborn, handicapped and elderly. Hope may be forgotten by some but it will always be held high by others, not in a foolish optimism that avoids the cruel reality of today but with an intuitive faith in the opportunity of tomorrow. As the Psalmist of the Hebrew Scriptures writes (Psalm 42:6):

> *Why so downcast, my soul?*
> *Why do you sigh within me?*
> *Put your hope in God: I shall praise him yet, my*
> *Savior and my God.*

Creativity

Thus far, in this chapter, I have introduced you to the lifelong inner friends of Furious Love, Conscience, Courage, and Hope. Each of these attitudes are capacities of the spirit for building up life. I would now like to introduce you to and converse with the voice at the root of all the spirit's powers and capabilities, Creativity.

Out of the universal generative force of love, you were created as a image of God. At the very foundation of your being is a share in the power of divine creativity. As you were created, so you have the power to create. To the extent that you listen to Creativity's voice within will you be able to generate with love and create with benevolence.

> *The more faithfully you listen to the voice with-*
> *in you, the better you will hear what is sound-*
> *ing outside. And only he who listens can*
> *speak.*[11]

You are capable of generating because you have been created by the universal power of giving. As you have been given to, so can you give. As you have been healed, so can you heal. As you have been spoken into existence, so can you express your true self through the voice of the Creative One. The power of creativity is the power for life. It is not a competitive voice as many other feelings are. Creativity is rather a harmonious power that can integrate all the other passions of the soul and emotions of the heart. The voice of creativity can speak through a feeling of anger to build a stronger relationship, or express itself through the voice that speaks for a better life. Creativity is the power of giving, not of control, domination, or oppression.

When I look back on my life, my happiest moments were when I gave something to another, did something to make life a bit more beautiful or complete, or hesitated to do something that would hurt or harm another. I have felt most fulfilled when I have chosen to put aside my conflicting and nagging selves and let the creative power of generosity flow through me. It is when I give that I receive. Norman Cousins affirms this essential point:

> *No one need fear death. We need fear only that we may die without having known our greatest power—the power of our free will to give our life for others. If something comes to life in others because of us, then we have made an approach to immortality.*[12]

Conversation with Creativity

J.P. You are the one voice I long to hear and seek to follow, yet you are also the voice that demands the most of me. Of all the inner voices, you demand the most difficult work.

CREATIVITY I don't demand that you listen to me. That's up to you. I certainly want to entice you as I speak of the happiness that's possible if you will but follow me, but I have no power to demand that you face reality. If you want to live addicted to feelings of resentment and guilt, even to a substance or person, that's up to you. When you choose not to be creative, you create any way out of your passivity. In order to self-create, you must face the reality of your many divided selves, discipline your selves with love, and let go of your fear.

J.P. You are terrifying, yet at the same time you have a wondrous power. You cause me the greatest suffering, yet also the most profound joy.

CREATIVITY Nothing seems to hurt so much as learning how to give. You must first let go of your desire to take and manipulate. In the long run, you know that selfishness will never bring you the peace you so deeply desire. Only creative giving can reward you with serenity. I know that what I say is difficult for you to understand, birth is always more difficult than death; creating is always more work than living a passive and possessed lazy life of fear.

J.P. But what more can I do? I only have so much talent, so much time. I can only give so much before I am consumed.

CREATIVITY That line about limited talents and little time is a common excuse. The only reason you refuse to give is because you're afraid of losing the comfort you've acquired. You can't create out of nothing, only the divine creator can do that. However, you can create with the energy you've tied up in fear and imprisoned in anger. You have to die a bit in order to be re-born; that's what you're afraid of. You must let go in order to be transformed.

J.P. I am not always possessed by fear. I've given you some freedom. I've struggled and sacrificed enough to know not only that you're the deepest part of my identity, perhaps the closest to God of my many selves, but I also know that my life has not been wasted. I've accomplished much along the way. I'm not totally enslaved to selfishness.

CREATIVITY I know. I'm not accusing you. Don't be so defensive. You've come a long way toward freeing me to flow through you, but that's not enough. You still play it too safe. You give, all right, but frequently only on your terms, when the cost is not too high, the risk not too great. If you stick with me, it's going to cost you much more than you are usually willing to pay.

J.P. I don't know what to say. How can I be more creative, more giving, than I have been already?

CREATIVITY Perhaps you could work a bit more earnestly at re-creating your inner family and community. Perhaps you could spend a bit more time each day in dialogue with your selves so that your one true self in God could have a chance to speak. This is just a suggestion, but perhaps you could generate new life within prayer. Who knows who or what may be born within if you but cooperate with the eternal power of creativity. Perhaps even God might be incarnated within if you open your heart to such a possibility. I know this means that some of your selves will have to die so that God can be born in you, but that's the price for true and honest generosity.

J.P. I'm a bit surprised at your answer. I thought you were going to tell me how I can be more creatively generous with others.

CREATIVITY That's exactly what I told you. Perhaps I can put it another way. If you re-create your inner family around divine creativity, you will be a generative force in your family, neighborhood, and country. Only when you're reborn in compassion can you show compassion to others.

J.P. Perhaps we'd better leave this conversation for another time, my friend. I know you're trying to free me for a fuller, creative life, but I'm beginning to get a bit confused. Perhaps we should pick up this discussion again later.

CREATIVITY I look forward to any future conversation you'd like to have. In fact, the entire inner family has been profoundly moved by these recent conversations. We certainly hope that the communication will continue.

Communicate or Bust

A number of years ago, I sat with a close friend and spiritual guide for what turned out to be our last moments together. Within weeks of our conversation, he would die very suddenly. However, my wise friend told me something that continues to echo within my soul. I believe that to a large extent this book is a response to what my friend said to me during that fateful and loving dialogue. "John," he said, "you have an awful lot to give, an awful lot to say. You had better find a way to get it out or you will go mad."

Creativity needs a way out from under the pall of fear, a path to communicate and express its life-transforming energy. The path of communication is not as important as the fact that you speak your words of love, dance your message of beauty, mold your inner voice in clay, paint your visions in a variety of color, play the piano keys in tones of hope, write your words in pages filled with ideas, embrace your child or spouse in a tender touch, reveal your care by just sweeping a broom across the floor, or by marching long roads for justice. Communicate or go mad; give or die.

> *Vulnerability is no excuse for not creating, just as fear is no excuse for lack of courage, and despair, no excuse for lack of hope. Fear produces courage which, in fact, happens in the midst of fear. Despair produces hope, which is born in the depths of despair, and vulnerability produces creativity, which requires a capacity to get hurt.*[13]

Those who have the most to say and should be heard are those who have been hurt the most and yet love, those who have suffered most yet who continue to give, those who have sacrificed most yet continue to share. What they have to say can have the creative power to transform society. . .if we will only listen.

Is That All There Is?

Thus far I have introduced and talked with a number of inner feelings, which you can either make into enemies or friends. I have also called forth from the inner family a few of the lifelong friends we all share. But is that all there is? Is the purpose of our lives locked in some battle between competing voices of goodness and evil? Are we trapped in an isolating world of opposition where we choose what we will become by identifying more with this or that feeling, this or another attitude?

To some extent, it is true that you create yourself by the choices that you make. It is true that:

> *Each individual is capable of both great altruism and great venality. He has it within his means to extend the former and exorcise the latter.*
>
> *The individual is capable of both great compassion and great indifference. He has it within his means to nourish the former and outgrow the latter.*
>
> *The individual is capable of maintaining great societies and staging great holocausts. He has it within his means to fortify the former and avert the latter.*
>
> *The individual is capable of ennobling life and disfiguring it. He has it within his means to assert the former and anathematize the latter.*[14]

However, am I not more than the identity I choose? Dag Hammarskjold answers this question in this insightful passage:

> *At every moment you choose yourself. But do you choose "your" self? Body and soul contain a thousand possibilities out of which you can build many I's. But in only one of them is there*

congruence of the elector and the elected. Only one—which you will never find until you have excluded all those superficial and fleeting possibilities of being and doing with which you toy, out of curiosity or wonder or greed, and which hinder you from casting anchor in the experience of the mystery of life, and the consciousness of the talent entrusted to you which is your I "self."[15]

There is more to my inner family than just positive powers, no matter how well intentioned, and negative voices, no matter how destructive. There is more to inner peace than just accentuating the psychologically positive. There is a deeper source of serenity, a will higher than my own, a central power of purpose around which my inner family can gather in harmony. There is a self I can call my own, that will not change with the sudden shifts of psychological weather patterns.

In the next two chapters, I will introduce you to the Eternal Inner Companions that have chosen you. It is in and through the divine friends that you will experience supreme serenity and synthesis.

Chapter Five

The Centering Source

In the Thornton Wilder play, *Our Town*, as the wise Stage Manager guides us through the lives and deaths of the people of Grovers Corners, New Hampshire, he reminds us:

> *Now there are some things we all know, but we don't take'm out and look at'm very often. We all know that something is eternal. And it ain't houses and it ain't names, and it ain't earth and it ain't even the stars. . .everybody knows in their bones that something is eternal, and that something has to do with human beings. All the greatest people ever lived have been telling us that for five thousand years and yet you'd be surprised how people are always losing hold of it. There's something way down deep that's eternal about every human being.*[1]

There is an essential reality upon which the identity can be established that is not based on fleeting feelings or moods. Identity grows out of eternal truth not static security, out of everlasting being not temporary passivity. The truth of eternal identity will surely set us free for serenity, if we let go of the shallow images we create for ourselves out of fear and insecurity. The truth may seem hidden, but to find it we need only the courage to look behind the false selves we have built with such earnest. In the following story Piero Ferrucci tells us where the eternal truth of identity and serenity can be found.

One day, according to an eastern story, the gods decided to create the universe. They created the stars, the sun, the moon. They created the seas, the mountains, the flowers, and the clouds. Then they created human beings. At the end they created truth.

At this point, however, a problem arose: where should they hide truth so that human beings would not find it right away? They wanted to prolong the adventure of the search.

"Let's put the truth on top of the highest mountain," said one of the Gods. "Certainly it will be hard to find it there." "Let's put it on the farthest star," said another. "Let's hide it in the darkest and deepest of abysses." "Let's conceal it on the secret side of the moon."

At the end, the wisest and most ancient God said, "No, we will hide truth inside the very heart of human beings. In this way they will look for it all over the Universe, without being aware of having it inside themselves all the time."[2]

The truth of "who you are" lives within as the source and power of identity and personality. Serenity is discovered when you find, if even for a moment, the Eternal Truth, Source, Vital Force, Unifying Center, Higher Power, Imminent Intelligence, Numinous Mystery, Greater Being, God, Eternal Family, or the Divine Being within yourself. Among your many selves, but on a deeper and more permanent level, lives the power for life, wholeness, and harmony. What do we mean, then, when we attempt to describe this Divine Being? Karlfried von Durckheim responds this way:

Divine Being is an abstract and, as it were, far away term in relation to our conceptual thinking. But in the depths of our inner experience it is the most concrete and closest to us. It is, after all, that with which, in our essential being, we are one; or to put it more clearly, it is that which in our being we really are. . . When we are thus seized by Divine Being, our basic mood entirely changes. Strength, joy and love seem to wake within us.³

The real purpose of life is to let flow the divine source within, to make room for the vital force and to manifest the highest power of love.

When you cling to a narrow and limited identity, holding fast to this or that feeling, this or that mood, as though in them you will find deep meaning, you blind yourself to the deeper reality of your true source and one true self. As I mentioned earlier, "dis-identifying" from limited self-images can set you free for an experience of the deeper self within. In the final analysis, you are not your feelings, even though they may ride you with wild swings. You are not your moods, passions, or attitudes, despite the fact that they come and go with ferocious impact. But if you are not your feelings and moods, who are you? Where can you find a sense of identity that will bring serenity as its companion?

True Self: The Power Within

In your truest identity, you are a concrete manifestation of divine consciousness. In your essential being, you are a spark of divine being with the will power to direct your life along paths that are positive and self-creating. You are a self, an expression of the source, a synthesis of body, mind, soul, and emotion, a reflection of pure consciousness capable of supreme awareness and choice. You are a child of God.

Inevitably, life is nourished by what you grant ultimate meaning to. If you allow your life to be anchored by fear, you will truly be limited in your potential. If you hold fast to a passive life without pain, you will surely limit your experience of your capacity for the divine. We are all inclined to cling to our feelings, thinking that they will remain forever if we protect ourselves enough from outer disturbance. We tend to build our identity on the desire for limited security, thinking it will bring us just enough peace to get us through the rough spots. What you center your life upon, however, is who you will become. If fear is your focus, it will control your identity; if security is your deepest desire, it will destroy serenity. Von Durckheim writes:

> Once a man is anchored in his essential being,
> he becomes aware that there exists within him
> a core that nothing can destroy—the true self.[4]

If your deepest desire is to know your true self and not just the selves that trap you in this passion or that feeling, you must first affirm the existence of a God not made by human needs. Only with God as the center, as the head of the inner family, will you be able to live with serenity in the inner kingdom, household, and community. Consider (Psalm 139:13-14):

> It was you (God) who created my inmost self,
> and put me together in my mother's womb; for
> all these mysteries I thank you: for the wonder
> of myself, for the wonder of your works.

Centering Experience

In an earlier chapter, I described a personal retreat experience during which I was asked to look within and draw my innermost images, whether angels or false gods. I would like to return to that retreat experience now to complete the story.

Analyzing your behavior and inner dynamics is never easy. It is perhaps life's most difficult task. Admitting to yourself that you are controlled by fear, dominated by anxiety, ruled by guilt, or even perhaps more difficult, recognizing your capacities for love, joy, and creativity is a process that demands a great deal of honesty. During my retreat experience, I was able, with a great deal of help from my guide, to name some of the enemies I had created and some of the friends that I had been gifted with. Not only did I try to name Fear, Inner Manipulator, Guilty One, Innocent One, Angry One, and Creative One, I also tried to draw each on a separate piece of paper. By the end of my retreat, I had sketched some sixteen sub-personalities or limited selves. Some were pictures of feelings I gave power to; others were drawings of roles I played. There was much more I could have seen and perhaps should have imaged in the drawings, but my honesty went only so far on that particular challenging journey within.

There was an afternoon during the final day of my retreat experience, however, when it finally came time to stop analyzing. I knew there had to be a time when I would stop taking myself apart in order to begin putting my selves together again. It was then that my spiritual guide joined me for a session of synthesis. My task during this therapeutic session was to show each drawing of my many selves to my guide, to describe each, and to answer any questions put to me. It was an experience I hope I will never forget. After I introduced and described a sub-personality to my guide, he would tell me to place it on the floor. Eventually the sixteen drawings of my many selves formed a circle around a small table in the middle of the room. When the circle was complete, my guide simply said, "Now it is time to celebrate the Eucharist. The altar will be this small table, the congregation, your many inner selves." At this sacred service of

synthesis, the following words of Christ were read:
"Where two or three meet in my name, I shall be there
with them" (Matthew 18:20).

Never before had I been so overwhelmed by a sense
of unity, completeness, and peace. As I sat in the center
at the small table and breathed the power of the Source,
I was nourished with the eternal food only the Source
can give. It was during this religious ceremony, as I con-
templated my many selves and celebrated the only eternal Source and foundation of my self and soul, that I also
heard Dietrich Bonhoeffer's ultimate answer to the basic
question he posed in our first chapter:

> *Who am I? They mock me, those lonely ques-*
> *tions of mine. Whoever I am, thou knowest, O*
> *God, I am thine!*[5]

The Divine Noise

You will never find true serenity if you do not come
to know and listen to the divine being within. Without
God, you may know and achieve some inner balance, but
it is a temporary condition based on dominance. Peace
without God is merely a static sense of security achieved
by stopping all inner growth or movement. Real serenity
is experienced when the chorus of "I am's" surrender to
the solo, "God is."

Anyone committed to finding eternal truth is open
to hear the voice of Divine Being. From the holy dwelling
of the soul, the power for faith, hope, and love speaks in
whispers and thunders in challenge (Psalm 29:3-5, 7-8):

> *The voice of Yahweh over the waters!*
> *Yahweh over the multitudinous waters!*
> *The voice of Yahweh is power!*
> *The voice of Yahweh is splendor!*
>
> *The voice of Yahweh shatters the cedars. . .*
> *The voice of Yahweh sharpens lightening*

shafts!
The voice of Yahweh sets the wilderness shaking.

When you listen to the voice of your deepest self, which is forever flowing from God, you are strengthened with the power of confidence and love. As Dr. Gerald Jampolsky has written, it is by

> . . .*letting go of all distorted self-concepts that we can remember that the only real thing about us is love, which has always been here, the one Self that God created.*[6]

When you listen to the Source of your self, you hear the challenge of love, a love that can heal all inner division and brokenness. The voice of God has the graceful power to liberate life from enslavement to ego conflicts.

For those who have rationalized life as a game of getting what you can, afraid that there is nothing more than what can be seen, faith is a foolish stance, hope a mirage, and love a childish wish. Only the wise fools who believe in the irrational can participate in the strength of a power greater than themselves. Serenity is not something you get or achieve, but rather something you surrender your selves to. When you let go of the egocentric desire to be in total control and surrender to the power for life that is your Source, you discover the serenity that has always been there and will forever be there for those who have faith. In order to believe in your self you must first believe in a power greater than your many selves. Amid such faith, serenity will flourish.

As your many selves fight for control and compete for the center position in the inner family, the source within lives in a shelter of divine calm and strength. Peace may mean, for some, merely living without inner conflict, but for those who seek true serenity, peace means much more than the mere lack of inner hostility.

Living in peace with your many selves means living from
the center and manifesting the Source in words and acts
of love. To find one's self is to find God; to find God is to
find the grace of serenity and calmness that can shine in
the darkest storm. Listen to the music of the self and
you will know the tones of tranquility; listen to the noise
of the selves and the best you can achieve is a temporary
cease-fire.

> *Creation is nothing but a concert piece, con-*
> *sisting of representative repetitions, variations*
> *of and harmonious commentaries upon the*
> *simple theme, God, who is defined. . .as an*
> *Act. . .the Act of Love. . .the first step toward*
> *becoming able to hear it is to fix your attention,*
> *as every listener to learned music does, upon*
> *the theme, which is God, and "the love which*
> *is between Himself," the love of which all loves*
> *are more or less remote echoes and refrains.*[7]

Chapter Six

Guides and Eternal Companions

No matter how hard you try, you cannot achieve inner harmony around the Source without guidance. Whether your purpose is to find inner peace or merely to get through another day without tormenting anxiety or worries, you cannot do it alone. Whether it be the guidance of the inner Spirit, wise inner guide, Christ within or the mentoring of a significant other person, you cannot learn to live with your many inner selves without help. No one grows alone. Isolation is the enemy of emotional and spiritual synthesis.

There is a terribly erroneous idea to which many are enslaved that says that if you have a problem you must solve it alone. Showing the need for guidance is considered by many to be a weakness. Until the pain of living in inner conflict becomes unbearable, those trapped by the fear of what others will think will, sad to say, continue to keep any problems or concerns to themselves. Until you can rid yourself of the erroneous idea that there is something wrong with you just because you need emotional or spiritual help, you will not grow. Those who recognize their need for guidance have the opportunity to find deep serenity.

Dolores Curran holds that one of the most important characteristics of a family growing in love is the ability to recognize when guidance is needed.

The healthy family admits to and seeks help with problems.[1]

This positive characteristic is not only a trait of the healthy outer family of mother, father, and children but it is also true of the healthy inner family. There are no awards for those who try to make it on their own; there is only a sense of loneliness. There is, however, a deep and abiding sense of accomplishment for those who know that they are only learners on the inner and outer journeys. To those courageous enough to reach for help will be given the gifts of self-understanding and serenity.

Characteristics of the Guide

The person you choose and trust as your guide for the inner journey depends, to some extent, upon your need. If your inner family is at constant war, building to a possible inner nuclear holocaust, then a professional therapeutic relationship is certainly necessary. If you are being torn to shreds by fear or guilt, neurotically or psychotically destroying yourself, a trained guide of the mind and heart is essential. When you are beside yourself and unable to cope with feelings of depression or anxiety, then counselling or therapy is the best atmosphere and relationship for assistance. No one should deny himself or herself the strength of a trained guide because of what others will think. If you have grown emotionally ill because of the constant inner battle, then a physician of the psyche is required.

If professional assistance is not called for, despite its benefits, and you still desire a guide on the way toward unity, perhaps the best guide is already within you.

All guides know where they started from and where they are going. Guides worth your trust have mapped out the journey from experience. A guide for the inner journey, especially, should have traveled the roads within many times. No one can guide another who has not confronted the obstacles and seen the road signs on their own inner journey.

The best guides and mentors for the journey toward serenity, whether professional or not, have these basic characteristics:

1. Provides an atmosphere for communicating freely without preconceived expectations of performance.

2. Listens attentively with respect, mirroring what is said, for the sake of self-understanding.

3. Helps you confess your demons and baptize your hopes through honest self-observation.

4. Assists in the search for the source that gives ultimate meaning and purpose

5. Helps you realize and manifest the power of the source in your daily life.

6. Lets you choose for yourself the path you will walk.

Guidance on the journey toward wholeness is essential. No one is capable of making the journey toward emotional health and spiritual wholeness alone. It is just too dangerous and filled with self-deception. A trusted mentor is required for growth. Here are some of those guides you can place all your confidence in.

The Mentoring Christ and Spirit

The intuitive guide toward supreme serenity has been described with many images: teacher, mentor, observer, therapist, healer, guru. In the Christian tradition, the Source is God the Father; the supreme self is Christ; the eternal guide and mentor is the Holy Spirit.

The teaching Christ lives always within, leading the way toward supreme peace with God. It is Christ who can set the inner family free. It was Christ's purpose to teach the good news of salvation, to map the path toward a serenity that will last forever. In the Christian Scriptures Jesus declares his task when he says (Luke 4:17-19):

> *The spirit of the Lord has been given to me, for he has anointed me. He has sent me to bring good news to the poor, to proclaim liberty to the captives and to the blind new sight, to set the downtrodden free, to proclaim the Lord's year of favor.*

The inner Christ heals and forgives without possessing. He is the image of God made manifest as the supreme self of God, imminent within the human heart. He is the ideal model, the eternal example, the way to the source of God, the truth of identity, and the path to serenity.

Christ teaches the way and is himself the way to freedom from self-imposed limitations. He teaches that when you die to your many false selves you can live from the power of the source, God. By his relationship with God and by the example of his ministry, life, death, and resurrection Christ teaches how to let go of the conflicting inner selves that dominate us in order to let the true self and inmost being develop freely. He is the power of the Source of life, the Emmanuel, God with us, born in us to show the way to freedom.

The eternal guide is the Holy Spirit, who reveals that even God is a family of Trinity, dynamically related in love. As Jesus said (John 14:16-17, 25-26):

> *I shall ask the Father and He will give you an-*

other Advocate to be with you forever, the spir-
it of truth, whom the world can never receive,
since it neither sees nor know him; but you
can know him, because he is with you, he is in
you. . .I have said these things while still with
you; but the Advocate, the Holy Spirit whom
the father will send in my name, will teach you
everything and remind you of all that I have
said to you.

For those who recognize the Spirit of God and
Christ as the wise guide, prayer is a place of therapy and
development. The Spirit is an instructor in the ways of
Christ and in the teachings of his love. Christ himself
prays for our personal and spiritual synthesis and for the
ultimate harmony of all creation with God (John 17:21):

I pray. . .that all may be as you, Father are in
me, and I in you; I pray that all may be one in
us.

It is the Spirit that "will guide you to all truth" and
"announce to you the things to come" (John 16:13). It is
the Spirit, the mentor and advocate, who will guide your
selves toward oneness with God. It is the family of the
Father, Christ, and the Spirit that will guide your inner
family to serenity.

The Disciples Task

Evagrius Ponticus, a fourth-century monk of the
Egyptian desert, describes the task of a student of the
Spirit and pupil of Christ when he advises the maturing
Christian to

. . .keep careful watch over his thoughts which
point to the demons which are present. Let
him note well the complexity of his thoughts,
their periodicity, the demons which cause
them, with the order of their succession and

*the nature of their associations. Then let him
ask from Christ the explanations of these data
he has observed.*[2]

To follow the guidance of the Spirit toward harmony, you must discipline your selves, your feelings, desires, and passions. You must put on them "the bridle of love," as Matthew Fox describes:

*What is a bridle of love? A bridle is a steering
instrument. We are to steer, not control or
abuse; our passions. We are to make them work
for us, to discipline them, so that they take us
where we need to go, as is the case with a
bridle on a charging horse.*[3]

If you seek higher levels of supreme serenity with God, you must first become a disciple of Christ and the Spirit. On such a divine path you will surely experience power for life, power with life, and power toward a fuller life. Once experienced, such power must be shared with others.

Chapter Seven

Greater Family Unity

Up to this point the purpose of this book has been to promote a greater self-analysis for the purpose of personal and spiritual synthesis and serenity. Such a process is challenging, demanding at times every ounce of psychic and spiritual energy that the heart, soul, and body can muster. However, peace among the inner family members and spiritual serenity are not the ultimate goal of life.

Self-acceptance has as its ultimate purpose self-transcendent. If all you do is look within, merely to live with your selves with a greater sense of comfort, then you have missed the point of this book and of life. Inner serenity should be sought, yes, but for a higher and more wholesome goal: outer serenity. The honest struggle within for freedom gives courage for the outer struggle. Once you discover the true self, Christ, who is at the center of your being, you must share that self-discovery with others. In fact, when you authentically realize the power of Christ within, you are compelled to share it.

Since everyone is a part of the human family, we cannot find our self or Source apart from the rest of humanity; meaningful existence cannot be achieved in isolation from the larger community. Inner family harmony has as its primary purpose serenity in the community.

Communication within promotes more meaningful communication between people and nations and groups. The more you talk to your selves and listen to them, the more you are able to talk with and listen to others. The ultimate reason for working hard to get along with your selves, and the self of God within, is so that you can better get along with and relate more honestly to other people, while helping them to do the same. Inner health exists for outer health.

People want to get along with others, to live more peacefully, to work toward a greater harmony among diverse and competitive community groups. The problem is that we get so caught up in our own inner struggles that we forget how to relate to our brothers and sisters. We get in our own way, with our petty attachments and narrow ego-identifications, that we forget how to be with and for other people. We become so concerned with our inner peace and comfort that we ignore the greater needs of the larger community.

There is a basic tendency in each of us toward synthesis, sharing, and unity. In every living organism there is a driving urge to link up, to form networks, to be integrated and galvanized. Every maturing person prefers peace over conflict, serenity over mere security. Deep within is the desire for social and family unity. The only people who strive to dominate others, are those who have silenced within themselves the most basic human inclination: to live with others, empower others, and love others.

Principles

There are three essential principles concerning the relationship between inner family growth and harmony, and outer family growth and harmony.

Principle 1 The way you live with your inner selves is the way you will live with other people.

If your inner life is a constant and bitter struggle with opposing forces vying for control, then more than likely your outer relationships will be marked by competition and fighting. Inner fighting leads to outer fighting. How you relate to your inner family members is reflected in how you relate to your outer community members. The former Secretary General of the United Nations, U Thant, has noted:

> We cannot end the war between nations unless we end the war in the hearts of men.[1]

Inner serenity and security is a basic ingredient to right relations between nations, groups, neighbors, families, and individuals. If you don't get along with your selves, you will most likely find it difficult to get along with others. If you are your own worst enemy, judging and condemning yourself harshly, you are probably just as unfairly judgmental about the behavior of others, even though you may keep such negative thoughts to yourself. If you cannot accept and reconcile what you believe to be your own negative passions or thoughts, you may find yourself projecting them onto others. When you make enemies within, you also create adversaries in the outer community, to be fought, abused, or ignored. If you mistreat your inner family, you will mistreat the outer community.

If, however, you honor, accept and cherish your many inner selves, you will respect the dignity and rights of others. If you have not befriended inner feelings, then how can you take part in the building up of an open and peaceful society? If you ignore your own rights, to live freely as you are in God, how can you do justice to the rights of others?

It is only through a long, difficult process of purification that we can be weaned away from our destructive self-concepts in order to provide the space for love to unfold. The only thing we have to give to others is our self, who we truly are, nothing more and nothing less.

Principle 2 The qualities you identify your self with are the ones you will foster among others.

If our identity is characterized by greed, that is what we will nurture among others; if we are possessed by fear, fear is what we will foster; if we are warped by the need for control, we will encourage manipulation and tyranny over others. To a great degree, you choose who you are and you establish your identity by what you identify with and foster.

Humans live best when they live by love. If you live only for yourself, that is all you will get, a lonely and isolated inner life of conflict. Love provides a healthy atmosphere in which our best self and the best in others can unfold. Love provides the strength and confidence needed to take a chance on loving others. It galvanizes the personality and facilitates unity among others. Love is, as Teilhard de Chardin often called it, "the totalizing principle of human energy." It can protect our true self, heal inner conflict, bring together what is broken apart, nourish creative living, free us from inner prisons, and melt inner obstacles. Love, in a word, can make you whole.

Divine love seduces individuals and nations toward a greater synthesis than either can create alone. It teaches each individual how to be a compassionate, healing, and just presence. Not only should our goal be personal health and happiness but also, and perhaps more important, social change and transformation. Inner growth helps nurture the seeds of serenity and liberation among those in need, among those who suffer from hunger, tyranny, and prejudice. When you live from the Source, you live not only for your self but for the many others you know. . .and do not know. Even the anonymous millions who live outside your small world can be touched by your compassionate energy for synthesis and sharing.

As individuals, we must struggle to end the "divided house" of conflicting goals, wishes and desires within our personal lives. We must struggle to harmonize and integrate our many sub-personalities—the local dominions within ourselves—whose conflicts dissipate our energy by preventing its effective focusing and expression. The same is true with nations. For example, divided energies in the national life may be represented by the many internal groups which have different and conflicting values, concepts or goals. Thus, the energy of an ethnic or minority group, which has urgent unmet needs, will be largely lost to the nation until that group is accommodated and its reasonable needs satisfied.[2]

Prejudice based on race, sex, wealth, and religion separate the human family into camps of "right" and "wrong" powerful and powerless. The desire to be right destroys the urge for serenity; the need to be in control oppresses the possibility of greater unity. To paraphrase Marilyn Ferguson:

You are not liberated until you liberate others. So long as you need to control other people, however benign your motives, you are captive to that need. Giving them freedom, you free yourself.[3]

When you live from the power of the Source, social change is a primary task. Working for justice becomes a value with greater purpose than mere inner comfort. There is, however, another basic principle that ties the circle of serenity, self, God, and others together.

Principle 3   You cannot be a resource for real change in society until you begin the work of inner transformation.

No one has the power to change other people. You can effect an atmosphere in which others can choose to grow and prosper in justice, but you cannot force change in others, no matter how much you try. Love never pressures with shame or demands with blame. Rather, it shows itself through seductive examples of what peace and compassion can accomplish. It is not a power *over;* it is rather a power *for.* The most effective way to teach others the supreme value of love is by being a loving example in your daily life. Nothing teaches more and effects more community transformation than a consistent example of service, which is love in action.

Desiring social change and growth, however, is never quite enough. Once that is desired, you must work for justice, stand up for others' rights, and proclaim the dignity of each person, not because you are better than others, but because you are their equal in all things, including the power to love.

The only way you can change the world into a place where love and serenity can prosper is by changing the way you relate to your self. If you foster inner growth, the atmosphere you create around you will nurture freedom and serenity.

Perhaps the prayer of this sufi and teacher could be a common prayer for change.

I was a revolutionary when I was young and all my prayer to God was: "Lord, give me the energy to change the world."

As I approached middle age and realized that half my life was gone without changing a single soul, I changed my prayer to: "Lord, give me the grace to change all those who come in contact with me. Just my family and friends, and I shall be satisfied."

Now that I am an old man and my days are

numbered, I have begun to see how foolish I have been. My one prayer now is "Lord, give me the grace to change myself." If I had prayed for this right from the start I should not have wasted my life.

Everybody thinks of changing humanity.

Hardly anyone thinks of changing himself.[4]

Speak From the Source

Throughout this book, I have encouraged a deep self-study of what we base our identity on. We listened to and talked with some of our many inner selves, both our positive and negative voices. We have also heard the voice of God within who calls us toward inner and outer serenity. Listening to God is not enough, however. When you have heard the voice of God, you are compelled to proclaim it from the rooftops. Only when you speak from the power of the center, from deep within, can you share tranquility, build serenity, and foster confidence in the possibility of achieving fuller harmony.

Serenity can always increase; it can never be complete. Serenity can never be achieved as an isolated "I"; it can only striven for by "we," the family. What "we" can do together—self, others, and God—is far greater than "I" can ever do. If I do my part within through listening, self-study, inner dialogue, prayer, and letting go, God, the source of all serenity and love, will unfold through me, using me as a voice for greater outer family harmony.

Chapter Eight

Twelve Steps Toward Serenity

As I learn to communicate with my inner family listening, talking, praying, and sharing I will be able to hear the voice of the higher power which, if I am attentive and willing enough, will speak through me. What I have described in these pages is a process of a lifetime, the dynamic of growth and rebirth. The process of developing serenity can be described as a spiral that progresses toward higher levels of consciousness or as a plateau upon which greater love can be built. It is preferable to describe the process of emotional and spiritual growth and synthesis as a never-ending story.

I believe serenity is another word for heaven. Serenity already is heaven, and it grows stronger every day as we gather around the source of all reality, God. If heaven is mere security is that enough? It may be more painful and demand our courage, but it is also more rewarding to believe that all the way to serenity is serenity, just as for St. Catherine of Siena, "All the way to heaven is heaven."

A sense of calm unfolds when you come to believe that tomorrow will be another day for growth and that all the battles within and without do not have to be won today, that "winning" isn't everything. Surrendering to the self of God is much more courageous and rewarding.

Gathering Together

In an attempt to gather together much of what I have written, I conclude with a paraphrased list of twelve steps. If practiced as a way of life, these can help you befriend your many inner selves and enable you to live more sincerely. Living according to these steps every day can lead you to greater maturity, happiness, synthesis, and holiness.

1. I admit that I am often powerless over negative feelings, needs, desires, substances, and ideas, and that my life becomes unmanageable when I give my power to make decisions over to any part of myself.

2. I believe that a power and source greater than my many inner and outer selves can restore me to sanity and serenity.

3. I will continue to let my will be guided by the power for life, the Source of my understanding.

4. I will continue self-study, inner communication, honest self-analysis, making a fearless moral inventory of my inner demons, so that my inner friends and eternal companions can be liberated.

5. I will admit to my self, and to other significant people the exact nature of my wrongs, so that I can be guided by their forgiveness and wisdom.

6. I will center my true self and many false selves around God the Source and true motivator of life.

7. I will strive to recognize the truth about my

selves, humbly asking God, the Source, to forgive, heal, and lead the way.

8. I will admit when my self-destructive behavior hurts others and I will make amends.

9. I will sincerely and respectfully serve those whom I have hurt by my self-centeredness.

10. I will talk to and listen to my inner selves, taking inventory of the voices of negative emotions, desires, ideas, or needs, promptly admitting the presence of God, the Source, who can break through with love.

11. Through continuing attention I will communicate God through my every action and word praying also for the strength to accomplish the will of my true self.

12. As I awaken to the possibility of greater serenity, holiness, and happiness through the use of these steps, I will also try to share this with others, not through force but through daily practice and lived example.

Notes

Chapter One

1 Dietrich Bonhoeffer, *Letters and Papers from Prison* (New York: Macmillan Co., 1965), p. 221.

2 David Harden, *Images of Self-Recognition* (New York: Seabury Press, 1977), p. 3.

3 Scott Peck, *The Road Less Travelled* (New York: Simon and Schuster, 1978), p. 243.

4 Quoted by T.A. Harris, *I'm OK, You're OK* (New York: Harper & Row, 1969), p. 1.

Chapter Two

1 Dolores Curran, *Traits of a Healthy Family* (Minneapolis: Winston Press, 1983), p.31.

2 Harden, *Images*, p. 2.

3 Coventry Patmore, *The Rod, the Root, and the Flower* (London: G. Bell and Sons, 1914), p. 166.

4 Carl Jung, *Modern Man in Search of a Soul* (New York: Harcourt, Brace & World, 1933), p.234.

Chapter Three

1 Aristotle, *The Ethics of Aristotle*, Book 4 (New York: Penguin Books, 1976), p. 78.

2 Gerald G. Jampolsky, *Love Is Letting Go of Fear* (New York: Bantam Books, 1981), p. 78.

3 John Powell, S.J. *Why Am I Afraid to Tell You Who I Am?* (Allen, Texas: Argus, 1969), p. 167.

Chapter Four

1 Norman Cousins, *Human Options* (New York: W. W. Norton & Co. 1981), p. 206.

2 Patmore, *The Rod*, p.40.

3 Cousins, *Human Options*, p.63.

4 Marilyn Ferguson, *Aquarian Conspiracy* (Los Angeles: Tarche-Co., 1982), p. 192.

5 Ferguson, *Aquarian Conspiracy*, p. 110.

6 Cousins, *Human Options*, p. 36.

7 Cousins, *Human Options*, p. 68.

8 Dag Hammarskjold, *Markings* (New York: Ballantine Books, 1965), p. 3.

9 Hammarskjold, *Markings*, p. 3.

10 Pierro Ferrucci, *What We May Be* (Los Angeles: Tarcher Co., 1982), p. 6.

11 Hammarskjold, *Markings* p.8.

12 Cousins, *Human Options*, p.43.

13 Matthew Fox, *Original Blessing* (Sante Fe: Bear & Co., 1983), p. 203.

14 Cousins, *Human Options*, p. 58.

15 Hammarskjold, *Markings*, p. 12.

Chapter Five

1 Thorton Wilder, *Our Town* (New York: Avon Books, 1938), p. 112.

2 Ferrucci, *What We May Be*, p. 143.

3 Karlfried von Durkheim, *Daily Life as Spiritual Exercise* (New York: Harper & Row, 1972), pp. 60-61.

4 von Dirkheim, *Daily Life*, p. 79.

5 Bonhoeffer, *Letters*, p. 222.

6 Gerald G. Jampolsky, *Teach Only Love* (New York: Bantam Books, 1983), p. 27.

7 Patmore, *The Rod*, pp. 108-09.

Chapter Six

1 Curran, *Traits*, p. 257.

2 Evagrius Ponticus, *Praktikos* (Spencer, Mass.: Cistercian Publications, 1970), pp. 29-30.

3 Fox, *Original Blessing*, p. 205.

Chapter Seven

1 Quoted by James Vargin, *Global Education and Pesychosynthesis* (New York: Psychosynthesis Research Foundation, 1971), p. 12.

2 Donald Keys, *Synthesis Journal* I, No. 1 (1975), 8.

Also by Fr. John D. Powers, C.P.

Holy Human: Mystics for Our Time

"If you are just beginning to read some of the church's mystical literature, this charming little book by Father Powers is a nice prelude to deeper studies. Most of us know of Teresa of Avila, and Julian of Norwich has enjoyed a recent revival; but some of these mystics of centuries past are relatively unknown—forgotten saints whose writings are just being rediscovered. The interview/dialogue Father Powers uses brings their thought quite effectively into our own very different times. Who are Hildegard, Mechtild and Jan Van Ruysbroeck? They are real people, both wholly and holy human."

Catholic Standard

"Father Powers has spent many years in the Passionist Radio and TV Center, frequently interviewing celebrities for media replay. With great creative imagination, he travels back in time to 'interview' seven mystics who have great ideas to offer men and women today."

The Priest

"*Holy Human* is excellent. Its interview form is creative and enlivening. Within such restricted space, Powers presents the essential teachings of his chosen mystics clearly. He makes them appealing to those in our own time who wish to learn prayer and Christian living from these models, so gifted with grace. I welcome this fine volume as a splendid addition to books on mysticism. It makes the mystical life approachable for all who seek it."

Sr. Ritamary Bradley
St. Ambrose University

"John Powers provides a whole gallery of 'holy human men and women of yesterday who have shown us how to climb the mountain of God that rises before us, with eyes that see in the dark.' His highly successful 'interviews' with seven mystics make them appear as the eminent guides they are, guides who speak to our own times."

Prairie Messenger

Paper, 128 pp., $7.95

Also by Fr. John D. Powers, C.P.

If They Could Speak

"Here 10 witnesses to the passion of Jesus offer their stories on how the crucifixion changed their lives and how that event should change the life of every Christian."

The Catholic Observer

"We sidle up to those less than saintly biblical persons or to biblical saints in their less than saintly moments, conversing with the sleeping disciple James, the despairing Judas, the mocking soldier, along with Mary the mother and John the beloved. We walk away, finding the saints more human than we thought, the sinners more saintly than we ever gave them credit for."

Carroll Stuhlmueller, C.P.
Bible Today

"Passionist Father John D. Powers has carefully selected 10 witnesses to the crucifixion of Christ, and he has given them flesh and blood, motivation and memories of that day. In doing so he has created a powerful method of self-examination for readers of this book. He's made each of his characters flawed humans who had just a rudimentary understanding of what was going on around them that day. *If They Could Speak* is rich in religious paradox. Each witness to the crucifixion faces his or her own quandary."

Intermountain Catholic

Paper, 64 pp., $4.95